THE IMAGE MAKER

DR. BRIAN SIMMONS

Tulsa, Oklahoma

THE IMAGE MAKER

The Image Maker by Dr.Brian Simmons
Published by Insight Publishing Group
8801 S. Yale, Suite 410
Tulsa, OK 74137
918-493-1718

Unless otherwise noted, all Scripture quotations are from the New King James Version of the Bible. Copyright © 1979, 1980, 1982 by Thomas Nelson, Inc., publishers.

ISBN 1-932503-12-9
Library of Congress catalog card number: 2003113840

Printed in the United States of America

Dedication

To my children and grandchildren
Precious and Delightful

Charity, Robert, and Aidan Arnold
Joy, Todd, Brianna, David, and Rachel Skeirik
David Simmons

You are my joy and His SPIRITUAL SEED

To each of you this book is Affectionately Dedicated

"Do not be afraid. I am your shield, your very great reward."
Genesis 15:1

CONTENTS

CHAPTER ONE

THE IMAGE-MAKER

"In the beginning God"

This is where we must all begin . . . In the beginning.

As far back as your mind can imagine; there is God . . .

Fully satisfied with who He is . . .

Father, Son, and Holy Spirit.

God **transcendent** and God **alone.**

But something is missing!

Somewhere in this time before time He decided to make the world. In His eternal thoughts, He knew it was time to act. It was time to bring into being a universe for His glory . . . Genesis is God's autobiography.

"In the beginning God created the heavens and the earth." This is the foundation of all Theology. He is the One and only God!

The Un-Beginning Beginning!

The seal of perfection is stamped upon everything God has done. The combined skill of all the greatest literary minds could never design a composition that equals the splendor of Genesis chapter 1. It stands in a class all by itself.

The purpose of Creation is to display the **glory of God.** We are able to see in the created order of our universe the awesome wonder of the **Maker of the heavens.** The universe is God's advertisement—the display of His glory (Ps. 19:1). The earth is not "mother earth," it is His footstool . . . and heaven is His throne. *He spoke it into being!*

We see God at the very beginning as **powerful, purposeful, wise, and full of glory.** Speaking the Word of Creation from His eternal dwelling place of light, He created everything from nothing (Heb. 11:3). Creation takes us into the mystery of worship . . . we have no answers to our curiosity; we can only worship. Man was made by God not to be a scientist, astronomer or philosopher, but a **worshipper** (John 4:24). We will never be able to take the mystery out of Creation, for a God who is incomprehensible in His greatness accomplished it.

Who is this God who speaks and the galaxies spin into existence? Who is this One who gives birth to time? Who is this Eternal One that is full of mystery and wonder? The Hebrew name for God is "ELOHIM." Amazingly, this first name of Deity in the Bible is a plural noun that suggests the Trinity. The Hebrew word for ELOHIM means, 'The God of power.'

Creation and the New Creation

The word "beginning" is actually the Hebrew word for "firstfruits." The Bible begins with firstfruits! God is bringing forth His firstfruits in creation. His very life will spring forth from what He creates. He pours Himself into the Creation as firstfruits of His eternal purpose for the universe.

In the activities of the six days of Creation, there is a clear picture of the spiritual work of redemption by our Lord Jesus Christ in bringing us to Himself:

"Formless . . . empty . . . darkness"
the SINNER (Eph. 2:1-3)

"The Spirit of God . . . hovering"
the SOURCE of LIFE (John 6:44)

1st Day **"Let there be light"**
the SPOKEN WORD (John 1:1-4, 2 Cor. 4:6)

2nd Day **"Let there be an expanse"**
the SEPARATION and SALVATION (Col. 3:1-3)

3rd Day **"Let the land produce vegetation"**
the SPIRIT LIFE of fruitfulness (Gal. 5:22,23)

4th Day **"Let there be lights"**
the SPIRIT of REVELATION (Eph. 1:17)

that the God of our Lord Jesus Christ, the Father of glory may give you a spirit of wisdom

5th Day **"Let the water teem** [w/life] **. . . let birds fly"** the SWEET SAVOR of WORSHIP (Song of Sol. 2:12)

6th Day   **"Let us make man in our image"**
           the SHARING of HIS LIFE (Heb. 3:1,14)

7th Day   **"God had finished the work"**
           the SABBATH of PERFECTION (Heb. 4:1-11)

Creation Morning (1:2-5)

The brooding Spirit of God hovers over the darkness of the surface of the deep. What a foreboding scene! Darkness and confusion cannot dwell in the presence of the Creator God. Chaos was turned into Creation's order by the wisdom and symmetry of the Spirit of God (Prov. 8; Heb. 11:3). Before God's Word is spoken, all is void and formless—**this is true also of you and me!**

God is never thwarted by chaos; it merely provides Him an opportunity for His power and wisdom to be revealed. The way God created the universe is the same way He makes us over into the image of Christ. Systematically, with the creative Word of God, He brings the beauty of His life out of our dark chaos.

This same Holy Spirit **"brooded"** over a virgin named Mary to bring His Perfect Man into the world (Luke 1:35). The word hovered can also be translated 'to brood,' or 'to flutter' (The same word is used in Deuteronomy 32:11). This reveals the Holy Spirit as the DOVE of Genesis 8:8-12 and Matthew 3:16. Another form of this word is found in Daniel 7:2 and is translated, **"winds of heaven,"** reminding us of the Mighty Rushing Wind that gave birth to the church at Pentecost!

The progress of Creation moves from the lower to the higher, from the darker to the brighter, from the evening to the morning. The Word of God puts light into darkness, land in the midst of sea, air in the midst of water, life in the midst of the uninhabited earth. God always starts with form, then fills it with FULLNESS:

FORM	*FULLNESS*
Day 1 Light and Dark	**Day 4** Lights of Day and Night
Day 2 Sea and Sky	**Day 5** Creatures of Water/Sky
Day 3 Fertile Earth	**Day 6** Creatures of the Land

In nature, it is first the bud, then the blossom, then the fruit. It is first the baby, the child, and then the mature adult. So also it is in grace. Step by step, God releases fullness into an incomplete form. Out of our immaturity, God's grace brings forth perfection. He that has begun this good work will bring it to completion. He is the Philippians 1:6 God! Just as God saw the completion of Creation before it was finished, God sees the image of Christ each time He looks at you, even in your immaturity . . . because,

God said, "Let there be light!"

God spoke light into existence. As this Word of Power was released from the Almighty God, the Universe began to expand at the speed of light; **and it has been expanding ever since.** Nothing can stop this Light! God's kingdom operates according to the principle of an endless increase (Isa. 9:6,7), not by a power diminishing over time.

Think about the power of that Omnipotent Word, and the uncreated wisdom behind it! The explosion of light is still racing through the darkness at the rate of 5.89 trillion miles per year! Darkness heard the Word of creation and vanished! God's thoughts had already shaped the largest galaxy and the smallest atom before they were ever created. With exquisite skill and creativity, God shaped all things by His Word and spoke them into being with intricate detail and skill (Heb. 11:3).

This Light God called **"good,"** or *"beautiful"* (Eccl. 11:7). He separated light from darkness, calling the light **"day"** and the darkness **"night."** This light is a picture of the Lord Jesus Christ, the Light of the World. When Jesus came into the world the Father said of Him, "I am well pleased." God called His True Light "good."

'Yahweh' Hidden in Genesis

The Hebrew verbs used with **"Let there be"**— **"and there was"**, are related to the holy name Yahweh. *"Yehi"* (Let there be) & *"Wayhi"* (and there was). This gives us the name Yahweh in the very beginning of the Bible! **Yahweh** is the **"I am that I am,"** the God who said:

"Let there be . . . and there was."

REMEMBER THIS: God can begin in the darkness and end in the light. It is not difficult for God to work where there is darkness, chaos, and confusion. Man wants to begin with light, but God begins with darkness . . . He will begin with evening and turn it into day. This is God's way . . . He's Yahweh all the way!

The Second Day (1:6-8)

On this second day of Creation, God parts the waters below from the waters above (Ps. 33:9,148:4). He stretches out this **"expanse"**[1] (atmosphere) and names it **"sky."**

The **"waters"** above are wrapped up in the clouds. God has preserved above us, great store-chambers of rain, snow, and hail (Job 28:22,23, Ps. 104:13). The height of the heavens reminds us of God's supremacy and the infinite distance between us. The brightness of the heavens reminds us of His purity and glory. The vastness of the heavens teaches us the immensity and grandeur of His majesty. He is the God of the heavens!

The Third Day (1:9-13)

Good stuff always happens on the third day! The earth begins as a planet covered by a dark, uninterrupted ocean. The Lord speaks and light shines as the atmosphere takes its place. God parts the waters and forms the oceans, lakes, and rivers by the *raising up* of dry land (Ps. 104:9). On this third[2] day God creates earth's vegetation.

The earth was RAISED out of the waters and clothed with life. In the place of desolation and death, life springs forth.[3] As the earth was formed, God brought into being a profusion of flora that could reproduce and cross-pollinate, but within limits.

"According to their various kinds." As the earth began to take on this innocent and distinctive character, **"God saw that it was good,"** or 'beautiful.'

Fertility is a God-created capacity. He is the author of life, fruitfulness, and reproduction. LIFE is in the seed. God's fruits all multiply themselves. The Hebrew for **"after its kind"** is actually **'seeding seed.'**[4]

[NOTE: The work of God at Creation involved three separations. He separated the light from darkness. Then God separated the waters above from the waters beneath. And finally, He divided the water from the land. Out of this separated, resurrected land, God brought a variety of life . . . and that was just the third day!]

The Fourth Day (1:14-19)

On the fourth day, our eyes turn to the heavens as the Father of Lights creates the great luminaries of the universe. God speaks, and the sun, moon, and stars are instantly created! What indescribable power!

> *"The heavens are telling the glory of God;and their expanse is declaring the work of His hand"* **(Ps. 19:1)**.

Everywhere you look you can see the splendor of this wondrous setting created by our Father for the objects of His love. Earth is unequaled in its uniqueness— the heavens contain the embedded codes of God's glory. Symbolic signs testify to His greatness and wisdom. This is the imprisoned splendor of God manifested in this sacred universe. For those with eyes to see, the earth contains a hidden dialect of the heavenly language . . . a language that one day would become a Man. When perceived, these covert codes inspire us to have fellowship with this Image-Maker.

It is more than a play on words that the *sun* is a picture of the *SON!* He is called the *"sun of righteousness"* (Mal. 3:2) who will RISE with "healing in His wings" to gladden our hearts and set us free. The sun is like a *"bridegroom"* coming out of His chamber (Ps. 19:4-6). At

Jesus' transfiguration His face shone like the brightness of the sun (Matt. 17:2). The *"woman,"* [church] of Revelation is clothed with the sun (Rev. 12:1). He is our *"Dayspring."*

The moon, deriving all her light from the sun, is a picture of the church reflecting Christ. The fountain of her light is hidden from view. The world sees Him not, but she sees Him and reflects His beams to a darkened earth.

The stars[5] are often used as a picture of believers or ministries who shine with supernatural light (Dan. 12:3, 1 Cor. 15:40-44, Phil. 2:15). **"And let them serve as signs to mark seasons and days and years."**

God loves to give us signs. Every day is a parable. The way the sun and moon and seasons change all paints a picture for the newly created man. The day becomes a hint of God's ways. He makes us young in the morning as the sun rises . . . we become strong and valiant at our noonday . . . we become gentle in the calm evening of our lives . . . then we hardly know it as the night comes and carries us away, waiting for the next-day-resurrection.

EVERY DAY IS A PARABLE . . .

Indeed, we are the lights God sets as signs to mark the movement into maturity. As we become His bright sign, we will begin to **"govern the night"** by facing the Son and allowing His undimmed brightness to shine upon us. So every day is a parable; every season becomes a journey into becoming bright **"signs"** in the darkness.

The Fifth Day (1:20-23)

The work of the fifth day is the creation of animate life. All life in the sea and the air were created [marine life and birds].[6] Can you imagine the delight in the Father's heart as He created the various forms of life? I bet it was fun.

This fifth day[7] reveals the work of the Spirit and the ways of God. On this day the dove and the eagle were created. The work of Creation proceeds from one level to the next, systematically, the work of God's order and life continues until the day of perfect rest . . .

There in the beginning of time, in the primitive garden, we discover the original plan—God desires to have one like Himself. The Image-Maker has a longing to share His great mysteries of eternity. The best is yet to come . . .

---

[1] The Hebrew is similar to 'spreading a sheet,' or 'drawing out a curtain (Ps.104:2).

[2] Three is the number of resurrection (Hosea 6:2,3).

[3] Also in regeneration, those who were dead in sins have been raised to walk in newness of life (Eph. 2:1-9, Rom. 6:1-11).

[4] The believer is birthed by the Divine Seed, God's Word (1 Pet. 1:23, James 1:18).

[5] Although it is not mentioned here, we see from Psalm 147:4 that as God named the "sun" and "moon" He also gave names to each of the stars.

[6] What is literally said in the Hebrew in verse 20 is, 'Let the swarmers swarm, let the flyers fly.' God creates and then releases His creation to fulfill their purpose.

[7] The number five is the number that represents grace.

"So God created man in his own image,

in the image of God he created him;

male and female he created them."

Genesis 1:27

CHAPTER TWO

THE IMAGE-MAKER MAKES A MAN

"In our Image, in our Likeness"

How humbling! God made all things without our help! On the sixth day of Creation, the animals, both wild and domesticated, were supernaturally created. Species of every variety filled the earth. How glorious and diverse is our God! What a world God created for us!

At last, God makes man in His own image. Everything up to now is just God preparing for the universe to hear this:

"LET US MAKE MAN..."

This is more than a hint of the Godhead. Father, Son, and Holy Spirit shaping man inside and out! We are made after God's kind. Imagine the Father's heart pounding as He considered the possibilities of His Divine Idea . . . Let us make one we can share our love with! Watch now as the Image-Maker begins His work.

The origin of man is strikingly different from the origin of animals. In Psalm 8, David informs us that man has been made a little lower than 'Elohim,'[1] our Creator! The phrase, **"in our *image*, in our *likeness*,"** speaks of both the outward and inward aspects of mankind. The image refers to something inward; the likeness refers to something outward. Every human being is made in God's image and in God's likeness.

What is this image? It includes personality, the capacity for worship, and the ability to make moral decisions, our conscience, and the ability to reflect God. Created as His image-bearers, all human beings bear the expression, the image of God. We are photographs of God. Our characteristics were meant to be copies of God's.

Because He desires to "give" Himself to you, He took His own nature and likeness and fashioned a creature just like Him . . . one He could love with unlimited passion. Together we are meant to enjoy each other in the warmth of mutual love. Freely and openly we can share our lives and express our hearts. This is the Divine Idea. You are a thoughtfully inspired image formed in His loving thoughts. You are the Divine Idea. . . .

Perhaps a flame of beauty surrounded Adam and Eve in their innocence and purity. Crowned with glory and honor, Adam[2] and Eve stood as king and queen over all Creation. A shimmering innocence was their only garment. What does it fully mean that they were made in His image? That **"image"** was fully expressed by the incarnation and life of Jesus Christ. *"He is the image of the invisible God"* (Col. 1:15). The invisible God became visible in Jesus Christ!

Since man was created in the image of God
And the image of God is Christ,
Man was created
In the very image of Christ!

The very life of man is a bit of God. Our Father now unites flesh and spirit, joining us to both worlds. Formed out of dust, yet receiving the breath of God. Man becomes the centerpiece of God's Creation. Made a little lower than angels, every human being has stamped upon him or her, the very image of the Triune God. What glory and honor is bestowed upon each one of us!

God had a lamb before He had a man. Jesus was the Lamb slain _before_ the foundation of the world (Rev. 13:8). God had our need in mind as He spun galaxies into the sky. Before the foundation of the world there was a slain Lamb (1 Pet. 1:19,20). The print of the nails was upon Him even as He formed the world. The hands that formed each person were nail-pierced. As Adam was shaped from dust, redeeming mercy was stamped upon him. The Marked Maker has held every life in His hands.

One day, this Creator came to be made in the likeness of man (Phil. 2:6-8). What a wonder this is! **"God with us"** means God has become one of us, a human . . . like His creation (Matt. 1:23).

This shows that human beings will be transformed into the full image of Christ. Because we have this divine life as a SPIRITUAL SEED within us, we can be—and we _will_ be conformed into the image of Jesus Christ, our Creator (2 Cor. 3:18, Rom. 8:29). Those made from His image and who believe that Christ is the image of God, will be transformed into that image! When we see Him, we will all say, "We are like You and You are like us!"

We were made to have fellowship with God. The **"deep"** need of God was to commune with His image-bearers (Ps. 42:7). The likeness implanted within us at

Creation was the capacity to live like Christ. He is our NEW SELF. We are daily being renewed in knowledge after the image of our Creator (Col. 3:10).

God honors man and woman by giving them charge over all the earth (1 Cor. 3:22). **"And let them rule."** As His representatives we were made to express God and to rule over His creation. Human beings were given this commission of responsibility, exercising dominion over every living creature.[3] This is so His IMAGE could be seen throughout all creation. God desired a ruling man, one to take dominion of the earth for His glory . . . only then would He be satisfied. But notice, it states,

"let THEM rule."

The dominion of the earth will only be accomplished as man *and* woman together exercise their proper roles and rule. God's *image* is reflected in both men and women . . . and so is *rulership*. There must be a joining of the male and female personalities to exercise God's ultimate purpose for ruling over His creation.

"God blessed them and said to them, Be fruitful and increase in number; fill the earth and subdue it." The Father's blessing was not merely for them to achieve maximum personal pleasure in the garden, but rather He told them to live generationally. They were to have children and extend the Garden-relationship to the non-Garden part of their world. They were to pass on the favor of heaven to the next generation. Their purpose was to build into the future and increase until the earth (the non-Garden) was subdued.

Sadly, Adam and Eve chose to live for themselves at the expense of the future generations. Yet the Father will partner with us to cause the next generation to surpass the one before it.

God **"blessed"** them, affirming them in love. The Father's blessing was upon man and woman. This blessing is what the heart cries out for today. We long for the blessing of our earthly father, but in reality, we long for the blessing[4] from the **One** who abides forever.

Perhaps this **blessing** on Adam and Eve gave them powers we know nothing about. Perhaps part of this blessing of dominion was the power to speak to the earth, and food would come forth. It was after the fall that man must farm and till the ground. . . .

The blessing of God is incredible. Do not underestimate what it meant for the Creator to **bless** man in the garden. As for God, His work is perfect. He sees all that His hands have made and declares it to be **"very good,"** even the work He is doing in YOU!"

Although God disclosed Himself faintly in creation,[5] He has fully displayed Himself in His Son (John 1:18). His NEW CREATION is the believing heart (2 Cor. 5:17).

The Seventh Day (2:1-3)

God can do a lot in a week! So perfect is God's handiwork! Nothing can be added to it . . . and nothing taken from it (Eccl. 3:14). The morning stars sang together on this glorious day! Like an artist finishing His masterpiece, God **"rested from all His work,"** setting apart the seventh day as a special day for Himself.

God did not *need* a Sabbath; omnipotence never grows weary (Isa. 40:28). God simply rests in Himself. This is His own Day, not because He is weary, but because He is satisfied.

This seventh day is a picture of God's satisfaction with the work of His Son. A **"holy"** rest comes to those who trust in Jesus and cease from their own works (Rom. 4:5). The seventh day is the realm of His fullness and perfection. God wants to make us His Sabbath Rest, His Holy Day. There are a Sabbath People in the earth today. They are learning to cease from their own labors and let God work in them both to will and to do His good pleasure (Phil. 2:13, Heb. 4).

Are you a Sabbath rest for God? Can He find a resting-place in you? God works in many, but is at rest in few. Where His will rules, there will be rest. If our will is in competition with God's, there will be turmoil.

This was the order: God worked then He rested, so God's last day of creation became man's first day. Man rested with God. In this realm of the Father's rest, man is able to work effectively and creatively. If we are outside of that place of rest, creativity is disturbed and man's work turns into sweat. But in the rest of God, there is never sweat or burdensome toil.

Man's work was an expression of creativity as he rearranged and joined together the natural elements of His Father's world. Creativity became an act of worship and God and man were joined in the garden. Not a forced-labor-camp (like much of the religious world) but a garden of pleasure where creativity flourished.

Humanity was given by God the keys to artistic creativity. Inspiration flowed through the first couple in the garden. They were not placed in an environment of heavy rules and regulations. They were given the power of purpose and the freedom to express that purpose through their work.

◊ Dominion was placed in Adam's hands. This is what our God desires, to dwell with man and be at rest with him. In this, man becomes one with God, dwelling with Him, resting in God's accomplishments. Within this Sabbath realm, all is of God. The Sabbath practiced by Israel was just a type and shadow of the reality of Jesus Christ (the True Joshua). He will lead us into that Promised Land of Rest from our enemies.

Consider the lilies (Matt. 6:28,29). Without labor or struggle they are slowly becoming more glorious than Solomon. Consider how they grow. They toil not. So, within you, the Christ-life springs up from the Divine Seed planted in our nature (2 Pet. 1:4). God's Sabbath is not a day, but the **fullness of Christ** (Col. 2:16,17)!

Regarding Sabbath keeping today, it is common to set apart the first day of the week (Sunday) to worship and celebrate the resurrection of our Lord. However, there are many sincere ones today in the Body who esteem Saturday as the Sabbath (Rom. 14:1-12). The "commandment" to keep the Sabbath was not given here to man, but to Israel at the giving of the Law at Mt. Sinai (Ex. 20).

One final word before leaving this Chapter. God had the church in mind even as He made the worlds. Could it be that the seven days of Creation speak prophetically of the history of the world and the birth and progress of the church? **One day** is like **a thousand years** (2 Peter 3:8). The seven days of Creation would be **7,000** years. . . .

- **Day 1** – God separates lights from darkness, a picture of the first 1,000 years of human history with the fall of man and the beginning of the conflict between light and darkness, God and Satan.

- **Day 2** – On this day the waters were separated. During the second 1,000 year period the waters of the great flood covered the earth as God begins again His new creation work in the hearts of men.

- **Day 3** – This was the day that formed the seas. The seas are often used allegorically in Scripture as the nations or peoples. In the third 1,000 year period God gathered the peoples into nations. *

- **Day 4** – The separation of Day and Night take place and sun, moon, and stars are placed in the sky. During the fourth 1,000 years the Sun of Righteousness was born on earth, and the apostles (stars) led the church (moon).

- **Day 5** – God creates the great sea monsters. During the fifth 1,000 year period the great world religions sprang up on the earth and ruled the 'seas' (peoples); including Islam, Hinduism, etc.

- **Day 6** – Man is created in the image of God. As the sixth 1,000 year period came to an end, the world will see a church arise that is recreated in His image and showing forth His praises.

- **Day 7** – God rests. The next 1,000 year period we will see the coming of the Lord and the eternal kingdom established upon the earth. The Lord of the Sabbath will come as King of the nations.

---

[1] The Hebrew word used for *"heavenly beings"* in Psalm 8:5 (NIV) is 'Elohim.'

[2] According to the Talmud, the three Hebrew letters of Adam's name represent the initials of three men: Adam, David, and Messiah.

[3] Man was meant to rule over **"all the things that move along the ground."** The **"serpent and scorpion"** are powers of darkness (Luke 10:18-20, James 3:7,8).

[4] The servant Father . . . the Hebrew word 'blessed' means to 'kneel before someone in the attitude of servanthood.' A God touching His creation and breathing into man His breath, kneeling to serve the creation He formed.

[5] Creation is but "the outer fringe of His works" and the mere "whisper" of who He really is. Redemption and the resurrection of Christ are "the thunder of His power." (See Job 26:7-14.)

CHAPTER THREE

THE CREATOR'S KISS

"The man became a living being."

God was ready to begin His Divine Idea. He had a man, Adam, formed of clay. God needed a vessel, a container to receive His breath, His very life. It would begin with a kiss. . . .

There was no grain in the fields for there was no rain . . . and no man to till the ground. The word for ground is *'adamah'* (similar to Adam). Before the earth could flourish under God's blessing, there must be a man to take dominion. The Lord created man to walk with Him and cultivate a garden. God made the earth to need man's touch. God and man were to work together to subdue, cultivate, and take dominion of the earth.

> *"The highest heavens belong to the LORD, but the earth He has given to man"* (**Ps. 115:16**).

God had not caused it to rain upon the earth. In Joel 2 we see that God's Spirit is allegorized as rain. God wanted to comingle Himself with man by His Spirit. God had not yet sent His heavenly rains, His Spirit, to the earth. When the rain falls, it soaks into the ground (dust) and mingles with it for producing life.

The rains will come someday. The former and the latter rains will fill the hearts of men and cause us to be full of God, full of His life. God and man will be joined together—singing in the rain . . . and working the ground for a harvest! There can be no rain until man tills the ground. If there is no rain of the Spirit, it is only because the soil of our hearts has yet to be broken open. . . .

Subterranean streams or a "mist" came up and became the water supply of the earth before the flood. Another accurate translation of the Hebrew word mist is 'enveloping fog, or _VEIL_.' God tore the veil and formed a man![1]

+ Body - **"formed the man from the dust"**

+ Spirit - **"breathed into His nostrils the breath of life"**[2]

+ Soul - **"the man became a living being"**

God, the Master Craftsman **"formed the man** (Heb. 'Adam') **from the dust of the ground"** ('adamah'). All of us were formed from the dust. This helps put our life in perspective, doesn't it? Our natural and chemical origin is that of dust or clay, not gold. We are to be vessels, not ornaments.

The _"breath of the Almighty"_ has imparted to us a living spirit capable of spiritual understanding (Job 32:8) and a functioning conscience (Prov. 20:27). The 'inbreathing' of God produces human life. This is what constitutes humankind made in the image of God. This Divine Kiss was the catalyst of creation . . . the breath of the Image-Maker. This celestial substance gave life, enabling man to live in a new dimension—able to be transported into the realm of God. In this spirit dimension, man would know fellowship and intimacy with the Image-Maker.

Taking a deep breath, a surge of spirit-wind exploded into Adam as Father kissed his son. Instantly, every portion of Adam's being was filled with life as celestial substance poured into the man of clay lying in the Creator's arms. Out of the dark shadows of non-being, a new life came forth and a spirit was created. Man arose out of his darkness into the majesty of the light of God's presence. Man was born into the Divine Idea looking into the eyes of the Image-Maker. The presence of the True God was our environment.

After Adam and Eve were formed, every human being receives the **"breath of the Almighty"** at the time of conception. We were all born in the intimacy and love of a creative moment. We look into the face of God, our Image-Maker in the instant of our birth. We have our Father's eyes!

God wants us to know Him! It was a face-to-face KISS that gave man life! We are simply jars of clay containing the treasures of Christ (2 Cor. 4:7). We are, on the one hand, clods of dust; and on the other, a ray from God. One soon crumbles back to corruption; the other a deathless being. One sinks to the level of beasts; the other brings the wings of immortality. May our spirits breathe after Him!

"Man became a living being" or a 'living soul.' The joining of spirit and flesh forms the soul of man. God's powerful breath went into a human body and a soul was formed . . . Adam was able to live by the breath of life, which is the spirit of man. Adam is standing halfway between two worlds . . . He has a body of flesh like the animals, but a spirit of life from God. The body links him with the created world and his spirit with the uncreated God. We have a vessel for our journey in time [body] and a vessel for our journey into eternity [spirit].

Have you ever thought of the immense job God gave to Adam? He was told to "fill" the earth, "subdue it" and "rule over it!" The earth is very big! What a task God gave to Adam. Would God give him a task he could not complete? No, God made Adam and gave Him the "breath of life"—a powerful anointing that exceeds what we know today. Before Adam fell into sin, great powers were granted to him. All of these powers were greatly diminished after the fall. They are still resident within man, but hidden and immobilized:

- **Physical strength** – Adam never grew weary. Only after the fall did God say he would "sweat" in order to eat. Adam was told to "work" the garden and take care of it. The Garden of Eden was not small—it covered four regions covered by four rivers!

- **Great intellectual powers** – Adam memorized the names of countless animals with all their subspecies.

- **Authority** – Adam took dominion to rule over all the earth. God would not have asked Adam to manage and dominate the entire earth unless Adam had the ability to do so.

- **Spiritual similarity to God** – Adam was made in His likeness and in His image. The fullness of this is not yet known.

Created to be a creator. God was inspired with an idea, then God breathed into man . . . He inspired man and gave the power to speak, to think, to plan, to implement, to create, to imagine, to build, to love. These are identical traits of the Image-Maker. God gave Himself to man. Our imaginations create our worlds. As long as God is the Source of this inspiration our actions bring pleasure to our Creator. Freedom as a gift from our Creator releases creativity into the created order!

Notice the new designation of the Creator—**"the LORD God"** (v.4, 5, and 7). Up to this point the name God had been used, now LORD is added. In the Hebrew this is 'Yahweh-Elohim.' The name Elohim emphasizes the power and deeds of God. Yahweh or Jehovah is His personal Name, revealing His Personality. God wants us to know Him for Who He is, not only for what He does.

Both God and Adam needed a partner . . . God needed a man to till and work the garden, accomplishing God's purpose for man—to bring forth fruit! But Adam needs a bride . . . a partner for life who would be able to live and move and have her being in him. So God gave Adam a job and a wife! All of this was to be a picture to Adam of God's yearning for a forever partner who will not just work for Him but love and cherish Him!

Eden—The Garden of Delight (2:8-10)

After God made Adam, He immediately gave him a home. Mankind's first home was the perfect setting for Adam—a model home—furnished with love, freedom, creativity—all in the environment of acceptance and peace. All was placed under Adam's custodial care.

The place appointed for Adam was not a palace of gold, but a garden. . . . Planted by the Lord on the third day. All that God provides for us is pleasurable. Eden means *'pleasure'* or *'delight,'* and is the birthplace of delight and desire. The whole earth was a paradise to man, a pleasurable garden—a wonderland. This is life in its highest perfection. Man and woman lived above sin, sickness, pain, and death. Eden's very name reveals God's nature of love and grace. Even the location of the garden was sweet, **"in the east."**

The Bible commonly uses "east" in connection with Jesus. The east is the place of the rising light. Every time man looks to the rising sun he is unconsciously reminded of his original home. Ezekiel says the Prince will come through the eastern gate (Ezek. 43:1-4). The wise men saw His star in the east (Matt. 2:2).

The description of the garden with numerous geographical references proves it was more than a mythical place—it was a real and literal garden. Notice the parallel between the **Garden of Eden** and the **City of God**:

Genesis	Revelation
The River of Eden	*The River of God's Throne*
Gold in the land	*Gold in the City*
The Tree of Life	*The Tree of Life*
Bdellium & onyx stones	*The Precious stones*
God walking in the Garden	*God dwelling in the City*

Eden, the Garden of God, is also seen in Scripture as a picture of our relationship with God. There are a people today who are being comforted and loved, making them like Eden (Isa. 51:3). In the Song of Solomon, the

Bride (the Church) is called HIS Garden (Song of Sol. 6:2). Overcomers are given the privileges of dwelling in a glorious paradise-like relationship (Rev. 2:7, 2 Cor. 12:1-4).

Eden is the Kingdom of God, the Holy of Holies, Zion, the place of His absolute Lordship. Though man was placed in a garden, he was meant *to be* a garden. Man began in a garden, sinned in a garden, and he was driven out of the garden . . . Then Jesus came. He went into a Garden as the Perfect Man and tasted the fruits of our suffering and pain (Matt. 26:39) that we might become the garden of His delight.

The trees God planted in this garden were the best, the choicest. Everything was a pleasure and delight to man, charming the eye, touching the soul. God is a **Tender Father** to His first son of the earth, Adam. On all sides, discovery and encounters awaited him. His environment was meant to disciple him in understanding and choice. With joy and gladness, Adam communed with His Maker.

God set man in a garden. Not in a factory where he was to toil, not in a **school** where man was to study, but in a garden—a place where life grows. Our life in God is to be a garden where beautiful fruit springs forth. In the middle of the garden God planted two trees. God put Adam in front of the *Tree of Life.* He didn't give Adam a list of commandments, but offered him living food that would sustain him. God's purpose for man is not *doing,* but *eating.* God presented Himself to man in the form of food, for Jesus Christ is that Tree (Ps. 1). He is meant to be the life and sustenance of all whom God has formed (John 6:57).

The tree of life is the Tree of God's **un**created life. Adam was created, he did not have uncreated life like God has. Eating of this Tree would transform Adam from the natural into the supernatural, from one created by God to one born of God. The Lord is giving Adam the opportunity to forsake his created life and unite himself with God's life and live in surrender to His life every day. By eating of the tree, Adam would daily show his dependence on God.

The Tree of Life was to be a seal to Adam, assuring him of the continuance of life and happiness, leading him to immortality and everlasting bliss. As the tree was planted in the earth, so the breath of the Almighty was implanted within Adam. The Lord planted the Tree in the garden, in the ground, in the dirt. What was man made from? The Lord wanted to plant Himself in the dust of Adam and become life within Him. A tree planted in a garden and God planted in man is the picture we have in Genesis 2. . . .

As the tree was to receive nourishment from the soil, so Adam was to draw life and sustenance from His Maker. Life for Adam would depend on what he did with the "Tree." Life for you and I depends on what we do with the Tree upon which Jesus died. Jesus Christ is now to us the Tree of Life and is accessible to those who come by faith (John 15:1-7, Rev. 2:7, 22:2).

The Tree of the Knowledge of Good and Evil

To eat of this tree would give man the knowledge of good and evil, but without the knowledge of God.[3] These two trees confront man with a choice, to yield to God's will with a YES in his spirit or a NO. Choosing to know *Him* or to know good and evil.

Man is not meant to covet knowledge apart from a relationship to God. He longs to be the source of life, virtue, and wisdom. As we come humbly to Him (our Tree of Life) He will feed us and guide us. His wisdom is a "tree of life" for all that take hold of it (Prov. 3:18). Seeking knowledge apart from Him will only reveal our nakedness.

The Cross is the Tree of Life

"The God of our fathers raised Jesus from the dead- whom you had killed by hanging Him on a **tree**" (Acts 5:30). "He Himself bore our sins in His body on the **tree**" (1 Peter 2:24). The Cross of our Lord Jesus Christ is spoken of as a TREE.

- The tree of Life was *planted by God* (Gen. 2:9). The second "tree" was planted by man ("they . . . crucified Him" Matt. 27:35). It was human hands, which Jesus formed, that shaped and erected that cruel cross on the hill of Calvary.

- The tree of Life was *"pleasing to the eye"* (Gen. 3:6). The "tree" on Calvary was quite hideous, shocking to the senses (Isa. 53:2,3).

- The tree in the garden *released sin and death* (Gen. 2:17). The CROSS brings life and salvation. By eating, man lost spiritual life; by eating he obtains eternal life (John 6:53-54).

- Both trees were *planted in a garden* (John 19:41). The first Adam and the Last Adam were buried (planted) in a garden.

◆ Adam, the thief, through eating of the tree, was **turned out of Paradise.** The repentant thief, through eating of the second Tree, entered Paradise. A thief is connected with both trees (eating of the forbidden fruit was stealing). Isn't it more than a coincidence that we find "*two thieves*" connected with the second tree also? Jesus used the word "Paradise" only here as he accepted the thief into His kingdom (Luke 23:43).

◆ Both trees were "*in the middle*" (Gen. 2:9, John 19:18).

◆ Both are trees of "*the knowledge of good and evil.*" The Cross is where we see the true knowledge of what is good and what is evil. Goodness was personified, and He became sin for us. Both holiness and wickedness can be seen as we gaze upon the Blessed Tree.

◆ Satan did everything he could to get Adam and Eve to eat of the first tree, but he does everything he can to *keep* mankind from eating of the Tree of Life, the cross of Calvary.

The Rivers of Eden (2:10–14)

This is the first mention in the Bible of the River of God. What a beautiful scene—a garden Paradise with trees abounding, and a flowing River! God wants a River to flow out of you and me, His garden (John 7:37,38). This was a supernatural river of life, four flowing out of one Source. Most rivers flow into one, this river flowed out of one. Jesus is the Source of that River of Life. He gives refreshment and satisfaction to the hearts of His own

(Ezekiel 47:1-12, Zech.14:8). There was one river with four branches that flowed through the Garden of Eden.

Psalm 1:3 mentions trees (men) planted by rivers of waters (a reference to Gen. 2). The man of Eden was also created (planted) by rivers of flowing waters. God made man out of river-soaked earth. In the heavenly Paradise there is a River that proceeds out from the Throne of God and of the Lamb (Rev. 22:1). If you follow the River to its Source you will find the Lamb upon the throne! This River is the outflowing of God, the Living Word (Ps. 36:7-9, John 4:14).

The Tree of Life speaks of the receiving of Divine Life, while the River of Life speaks of the outflow or giving forth of His Life. Nothing can flow out of the River that has not first flowed into it. We can only minister that which is flowing into us. Lord, make me a reservoir of this Divine Water!

PISHON (Ganges) = 'overflowing increase, flowing free.'
    Havilah = 'to cause to grow' (Ezek. 47:9,12)

GIHON (Nile) = 'bursting forth, turbulent water.'
    Cush = 'blackness'

TIGRIS = 'rapids, swift flowing.'
    Asshur (Syria) = 'successful'

EUPHRATES = 'rushing' or 'fruitfulness'

These four Rivers describe the ministries of the children of God, as they become the OUTFLOW of the life of God on the earth. All these Rivers combined make up the New Testament life (i.e. the four Gospels).

1) They will overflow the twisting and corrupt ways of man and cause the TRUE life to grow in overflowing increase in the earth. The land of sorrow will be submerged with joy.

2) They will break forth in the blackness of this world system with life-giving streams. The people of light shall encompass the whole land of darkness.

3) They will swiftly show the religious systems and earthly success to be the vain, empty inventions of men in comparison to the flow of life through the Son of God. The release of the River will bring Divine Life and release to the captives.

4) God's people will rush forth with true spiritual fruitfulness and touch all the earth with the Fullness of Christ.

---

[1] The word "formed" means 'to press or squeeze into shape.' We are truly the clay and God is the Potter (Isa. 29:16, Jer. 18:2-6, Job 10:8,9).

[2] Lit. the 'breath of lives' (life and the power to procreate).

[3] Satan's lie left out one crucial point… they would know good, but without the power to do it. They would know evil, but without the power to avoid it.

"In the river was found

Gold . . .

Pearls . . .

Precious stones . . . "

CHAPTER FOUR

GOD'S GARDEN OF DELIGHT

*"The Lord God had planted a
garden . . . in Eden"*

These precious materials are for the building of God's dwelling place (1 Cor. 3:1-15). Wherever the River flows, gold and costly jewels will be uncovered by its flow. Wherever the life of God flows within us, it brings in the *gold* of His Divine Nature. God's churches are to be *golden* lamp stands. The flowing of the River also produces pearls. A pearl is a transformed substance and is a picture of regenerated man (Matt.13:45). The durable and valuable onyx stone was likewise found in the river . . . God was generous to give these valuable treasures to man in the garden.

All of this is a picture of the image of God coming forth in redeemed man. The gold, pearls and onyx are all used in the building of the New Jerusalem (God's place of union with man). The flow of this Divine River makes us suitable building material for the habitation of God! Not only was the Garden a lovely place, but a land of rich minerals and potential wealth. What a generous Giver is our CREATOR!

The Old Testament High Priest would wear a breast-plate with 12 precious stones. The 12 stones of the breast-plate correspond to the 12 gates of the New Jerusalem. In the eyes of God, the breastplate of the priest was a *miniature* New Jerusalem.

In the New Testament we have the 12 apostles of the Lamb as the foundation stones of that city. In 1 Corinthians 3, the apostle Paul points to these three building materials used in building up the church. The gold, pearls, and precious stones—all are transformed substances. They point us to the work of transformation within the heart of man.

Oysters in the deep waters of death produce pearls. It is out of a wound to the oyster (a grain of sand) that causes its life-juice to flow around the wound and makes it a pearl. It points us to Christ, the Divine Wounded One who went into the waters of death and secretes His life over us (those who wounded Him) to make us into pearls of great price.

In Revelation 21 and 22, we see a city made from the same materials as mentioned here in Genesis 2. There is a River, a Tree, and a City. The garden has become a City of the Lord's dwelling. Between the Garden and the City, a long process must take place. The New Jerusalem will be a City of gold, pearls, and precious stones. In *Genesis* these substances are found lying in a garden, in *Revelation* they are built into a City.

The Garden of Delight

A garden of pleasure was prepared for Adam. Everything good and pleasing was placed there for Adam to enjoy. What a kind and tender Father is the Image-Maker.

God's intention for man is that he would be a gardener, one who tills the ground. Taken from the earth, he now is given the earth to till.•Turning over the soil is a picture of how man must guard his heart, his life. We must become those who have been loosened and opened to the rain of God. The TREE OF LIFE must be planted in the soil of the human heart! When God charged man to till the ground, it meant that the soil of his heart must be broken up and prepared for the TREE OF LIFE to come into him.

The Hebrew word used for "keep" the garden is actually the word used in the Old Testament for "watchman." Adam's role was to be watchman over God's creation. He was to keep the garden and watch over it so that the serpent would be kept out. Man's created role is protector, keeper—a watchman! Intercession is built into the heart of a man. God wants to redeem this and make His men strong 'keepers' and 'watchmen' over His work on earth.

Man was essentially placed on probation. God now appears as his Ruler and Lawgiver. The penalty for disobedience would be death; first moral and spiritual—and later physical death. If man had only eaten from the tree of life, we would all still be in the paradise of God without sin, sickness, death, and shame. How we have fallen from God's intention for us! What grace has been shown fallen man!

A wonderful freedom was given to man. **"You are free to eat from any tree in the garden; but you must not**

eat from the tree of the knowledge of good and evil, for when you eat of it you will surely die." Everything in the garden of delight was for man, his pleasure. Paradise was given to man. Eden was radiant. The landscape was filled with color of unsurpassed beauty. Eden's garden was a conservatory of the fairest vegetation and a storehouse of choice fruits. The only restriction was that he must continue to abide in the pleasure of God, eating only what was right and true.

God was not unkind or harsh; our God was gracious and generous to man. God alone knows what is good for us. To enjoy the good we must trust and obey Him. If we disobey, we have decided for ourselves what is good and what is not good, and therefore, we have made ourselves a god.

The Gift of the Bride

God considered the solitude of man and said, **"It is not good for the man to be alone."** God knew what was best for man. Man is a sociable creature meant for fellowship with others. "Two are better than one" (Eccl. 4:9). Moreover, how could man bring forth offspring without a counterpart? The Lord provides for Adam what he needed most . . . a partner, a friend, a companion (Lit. 'Completer').

We must remember that God did not just create individuals. He created community. From this marriage would come children, and from this family would come community. Man was made to be in relationship with others to fulfill the purposes of God. We were created with a need for others. . . .

Every wife completes that which lacks in the man. The Hebrew word for **"helper"** is also used to describe **God** (Ex. 18:4, Ps. 20:2, 33:20, 46:2, 70:5, and 89:19). We could never say that God is inferior to man, nor could we say that woman is inferior to man. Man was created so that he needs the help of a partner. The "image of God" is both male and female. The word **"suitable"** means 'equal' and 'adequate.' The woman would be an equal and adequate partner for Adam.

Neither Adam nor Eve had earthly parents. Adam had no one to "leave" in order to bond to his wife. Eve likewise had no mother or father to say goodbye to as they were joined in marriage. This shows that the husband-wife relationship is to be permanent while the parent-child relationship is temporary. Sons and daughters leave their parents to be united in matrimony. This first marriage of Adam and Eve demonstrates the primacy of the husband-wife relationship over the parent-child relationship.

Adam and Eve are a picture of a soon-to-be married couple . . . The Lord Jesus Christ (The Last Adam) and His **Bride**, the Church (Eph. 5:22-33).

Jesus Christ can truly say, "I love My wife." If it is not good for man to be alone, in need of a wife; then it is not good for Jesus Christ to be alone . . . He longs for a Bride that will complete Him! Without the Bride, there is something missing . . . something incomplete with our Precious Lord. The Creator longs for a Partner worthy to share His Throne. YOU have become that Bridal Partner when you accepted Jesus into your heart!

In the first three days of creation, it was God who called the light *"day"* and named the dry land *"earth."* Now Adam is allowed to show his likeness to the Creator by giving names to the living creatures. God supernaturally led the animals two by two to Adam to be named by him. The animals all loved and obeyed Adam for there was no ferocious beast before the fall. The lion was as harmless as the lamb. Man was given wisdom and insight into God's work and participated with God. By naming each creature, Adam took dominion over it. *When you have the power to name something, you have the power of dominion over it.* This showed Adam's superiority over the animals.

Everything was to be placed under Adam's supervision. God speaks and creates the universe . . . Adam speaks and names the animals. God is assigning to man the work of one made in His image.

As the living creatures came to Adam, he obviously noted that he, unlike all of the others, dwelt alone without a mate. **"But for Adam no suitable helper was found."**

Eve formed from Adam's side, is a glorious story of Jesus, the Last Adam (1 Cor. 15:45) and the Church, the Bride of Christ (Eph. 5:21-33). God caused the man to fall into a deep sleep (Divine anesthesia or trance). Eve was formed from a rib out of the side of Adam; not out of his head to rule over him, nor out of his feet to be trampled upon by him, but out of his side to be equal with him . . . under his arm to be protected by him, next to his heartbeat so to be loved by him. Adam lost a rib, but gained a wonderful completion by the woman. The woman was custom built by God. . . .

As the spiritual anesthesia wore off, God looked deeply into Adam's eyes to see his reaction to the new creation woman—God was not disappointed with his response. Adam smiled and said, "Thank you, Father." The Father brought her to the man as his second self. The woman provided a brand new perspective for Adam's world. Her insights and feelings opened up for him new realms of spiritual reality. He would never be the same. For Eve, as she opened her eyes to see herself reflected in the Creator's eyes, this must have been a moment never forgotten. Then she was brought to the new creation man and they instantly bonded as one. Two parts making one.

The Father gave His consent to this bride to become one with Adam. Marriages can be made in heaven! So it was with our Heavenly Bridegroom, the Lord Jesus Christ. Placed in the deep sleep of death . . . Out of His wounded side came blood and water that cleansed and purchased the Bride—bringing her to new life.

Eve was in Adam before she became the Bride; we were chosen IN CHRIST before we were born (Eph. 1:4). Adam and Eve ruled together over this paradise; the Bride of Christ will rule and reign with Him over a restored creation. The Spiritual Bridegroom and the Mystical Bride are the counterparts to this story. This mystery of Christ and the Church is deep indeed! Adam did not have a clue what this was all about. Yet the Son knew when the Father put Adam in a deep sleep that it was a preview of the cross and the Bride-to-be that would come from His wounded side.

Adam received her and said, **"This is now bone of my bones and flesh of my flesh."** This, in Hebrew means more than body, but also *essence* or *self*. Adam was saying,

'She is from my soul. She is all I wanted!' Just as man was made last of all creation, showing the honor and dignity of man, so the woman is made last. Honor is upon her as the glory of man (1 Cor. 11:7). If the man is the head, the woman is the crown. The man was dust refined; the woman was dust doubly refined. It took one verse to describe man's creation and six verses to describe woman's beginning. Adam slept while the woman was formed so that he would not claim it was his making or under his direction.

The image of God is upon both the masculine and feminine qualities—they were a King and Queen!

It appears from Matthew 19:4-6 that God Himself said, *"For this reason a man will leave his father and mother and be united to his wife, and they will be one flesh."* A man must leave all other relationships to form a marriage and cleave to his wife. The bonds of marriage must be stronger than any other (Ps. 45:10,11).

This bond or covenant is to be so secure that it is never to be divided or weakened by having other lovers (Mal. 2:15). Jesus also left His Father when He came down to suffer and die for our salvation. He left His mother when He was on the Cross, tenderly leaving her in the hands of His friend, John the beloved (John 19:25-27). Jesus left Father and mother to cleave unto His Bride.

Biblical descriptions of the life in the Eden Sanctuary are breathtaking. Imagine the Dancing God enjoying His son and daughter in a loving relationship as their Father! Nothing would hinder their relationship as part of the eternal Family. Their daily walks in the cool of the day would be occasions of profound pleasure, unspeakable delight.

Both Adam and Eve were naked and unashamed in the garden of Paradise . . . at ease with one another, without fear of exploitation. In their nakedness Adam and Eve walked majestically through the garden of delight, content to be creatures living in the comforting care of their Creator. No pride, no shame, no fear. They lived in the weightlessness of grace and not experiencing the heaviness of shame. Accepted fully and accepting one another they walked in delight and satisfaction with God and with each other. So the Creation story is complete. Innocence and beauty filled their days as husband and wife lived in perfect harmony . . . This is God's Plan.

The matrix of the garden was an environment of unbelievable delight and love. Yet it was in the perfect place that doubt was born. . . .

One restriction was placed on humankind. One reasonable, wise restriction meant to preserve and protect Adam's race. We did not make ourselves; we are responsible to our Creator to obey, to serve, and to glorify Him in all things. The command not to eat of the forbidden tree was given to emphasize the relationship man was to have with God. But the creature became self-seeking, independent, and self-willed. Consequently he disobeyed God and was plunged into the dark night of spiritual darkness and death.

Sin is now a universal sickness, passed on to every human being. *"In Adam all die"* (1 Cor. 15:22). As Adam fell, we fall each one. Our daily lives prove he lives in us.

Adam relives his life in every human being, until Christ comes to live through us (Gal. 2:20, Phil. 1:21).

The Temptation and Fall (3:1-7)

For the first time in Scripture we meet that mysterious one, the Devil or Serpent. His chief aim is to get between your soul and God, bringing doubt upon the ways and Words of God. He seeks to replace God in the human heart, substituting his own lies in the place of truth. It was Adam who gave the serpent his name (Gen. 2:20), as an act of taking dominion over God's creation. Adam took dominion over the serpent when he gave him his name. He held the power to resist and conquer the temptations thrown at him. We never have an excuse for giving heed to the devil's lies.

"The serpent was more crafty (shrewd) **than any of the wild animals."** This serpent was apparently a very beautiful creature[1] in his precursed state. Satan is called the serpent in Revelation 12:9,14 and 20:2. Lucifer was the first king of the angels. As an anointed cherub he was likely the worship leader of heaven ("guardian cherub" Ezek. 28:14). The name Lucifer means 'light-bearer or shining one.' On the holy mountain of God, Lucifer had access to the presence of the Most High, walking among the fiery stones. Under this flaming cherub was an innumerable company of angelic beings. Full of wisdom and perfect in beauty, with every precious gem as his covering, Lucifer was second only to God Himself.

Yet, his heart was lifted up with pride.[2] He determined to ascend into heaven and exalt his throne above the stars of God and become like the Most High. This was treason and rebellion on the highest scale. It appears that one third of the angels rallied to his support (Rev. 12:3-9). Because of God's judgment the shining Lucifer now takes the form of the serpent. This vile serpent is now ready to coil himself around the hearts of Adam and Eve.

Why does the tempter appear in this story? How did he get into the Garden? The only possible answer is that God allowed him to enter. He came with the permission of God to tempt Adam and Eve just as he came with permission from God to test Job. Mankind was being tested by God to see if we would love Him willingly and freely . . . Notice the steps that led to the fall:

1) The voice of the Tempter was heeded. **"Did God really say?"** Instead of, "Get behind me Satan" (like Jesus did when the Serpent spoke through Peter in Matthew 11:23), Eve listened to the Evil One who challenged the authority of Jehovah-Elohim. If the Word of God were dwelling richly in Eve's heart she would have answered directly, "NO, God is good and His love will give us all that we need always." The serpent always throws doubt into our heart, suggesting that God does not mean what He says. His Word had lost its proper place of authority in her life.

2) Eve added to what God had said, tampering with God's Word (Prov. 30:6). God's command was simply **"You shall not eat of it."** To this Eve added to what God had said with her words, **"Neither shall you touch it."** He had said nothing about touching it.

3) The lie is finally spoken, **"You will not surely die."** When we believe a lie of Satan over the truth of God, we are bowing down to Satan and making him our lord. God now is treated as a liar. This is what has

happened to fallen man! Note that the serpent's lie has to do with denying God's judgment. Even today this is a battleground in the hearts of fallen men. He wants us to believe that God will never judge us for our sins (Matt. 7:13-27).

4) The devil suggested that God was withholding something good for them. This was meant to shake her confidence in God's love. **"For God knows that when you eat of it your eyes will be opened, and you will be like God, knowing good and evil."** The enemy wants to tell you that God's plan is not grounded in love but in cruelty. 'How can you place confidence in one who doesn't love you? If he loved you, why would He prohibit you from enjoying such good things! He knows that by eating this tree you will become Divine!' The serpent was drawing Eve to be God's judge instead of His worshiper.

---

[1] The Hebrew word for "serpent" is *nachash*, literally 'a shining one.'
[2] Pride is now described as "the trap of the devil" (2 Tim. 2:26).

CHAPTER FIVE

FORBIDDEN FRUIT

"The eyes of them both were opened"

Ignoring the millions of blessings, Eve saw one prohibition and allowed it to be twisted into a doubt of God's care. Sound familiar? Satan will always tempt you to question the love of God your Father. Jesus is God who became a Man to prove His love beyond a doubt. It is time for you to KNOW and RELY upon the love of God (1 John 4:16), for this is where the serpent will strike.

The forbidden fruit is now looked upon, desired, taken, eaten, and given to her husband. This is how sin entered the world and how sin enters our heart. The *will of God* was resisted, the *Word of God* was rejected, and the *ways of God* were deserted (1 John 2:15-17).

Satan works from without to within, the reverse of God's ways with man. God always begins His work within the heart until it is manifest in a changed life. However, Satan works externally, through the bodily senses and emotions of the soul until the spirit is corrupted. The serpent is slowly winding his scheme around Adam and Eve until God's government is surrendered to his vile leadership.

Satan directed his appeal to:

- *"the cravings of sinful man"* (good for food)
- *"the lust of his eyes"* (pleasing to the eye)
- *"the boasting of what he has and does"* (desire for wisdom)

The appeal of sin is rooted in the cravings of what we cannot have, what pleases the senses, and what will make us wise and admirable before others. True spirituality is being content and thankful for what we have and living for what pleases God.

The serpent deceived Eve; Adam walked into transgression with his eyes wide open. Adam heard the command not to eat directly from God and knew the details, but Eve heard it from Adam (1 Tim. 2:14). Both ate of the forbidden fruit and were immediately plunged into spiritual darkness. By choosing the tree of knowledge over life, Satan mingled himself with man. We are no longer able to express God fully or take dominion over His creation; evil has taken dominion over us.

"Then the eyes of them both were opened, and they realized they were naked." Filled with shame, they tasted spiritual death. In a moment, the crown of God's creation became powerless, terrified creatures that were aware of what they had done. Their eyes were opened to their true condition; *"wretched, pitiful, poor, blind, and naked"* (Rev. 3:17). What sad fruit from the tree of knowledge! Their eyes were opened to see evil but they are without the power to avoid it. The age of innocence is now over. The discovery of their nakedness led to a self-effort to cover it: **"they sewed fig[1] leaves together and made coverings** ('loincloths') **for themselves"** (Gen. 3:7). This is the first record of man's effort to remedy his fall by his own devices. Every effort to remedy our condition is futile (Job 31:33). We try to cover ourselves with the things of this world (wealth, pleasures, and entertainment)—using anything to try to cover our real need before God. The Lord wants to cover our nakedness with what HE provides (by the shedding of blood).

Satan was speaking to Eve through the serpent (2 Cor. 11:3). Through deception Satan gained power over our race and he continues that power by deceiving us still. In the same way Eve was *"deceived,"* he would seek to lead us astray from a pure and sincere devotion to Jesus (our Life). May we not fall into that temptation but remain ever devoted to Him.

Jesus, the Last Adam, overcame the serpent in a garden. As He prayed in Gethsemane, Satan wrestled with Him. Sweating great drops of blood our Lord Jesus struggled through the night in prayer. He was heard by the Father and won the victory. Just as in the Garden of Eden, man was once again 'asleep' to what the enemy had planned. . . .

"Then the man and his wife heard the sound of the LORD God as he was walking in the garden in the cool of the day, and they hid from the LORD God among the trees of the garden" (Gen. 3:8).

Adam, Where Are You?

Hearing **"the sound of the Lord God"** (what would that be like?) and knowing He was near, they hid themselves. This could have been early morning, or early evening. It was the approach of a Judge that put them into fright, yet it was their guilty conscience that drove them into hiding. God came down to paradise, not in the flaming fire of His chariot with thunder and lightning—He came as One who still sought to be familiar with them. He came walking[2], not running; walking deliberately as One slow to anger.

God manifested Himself on earth to commune with man, but all has changed. They hid from the Lord God among the trees. Before they had sinned, Adam and Eve would have run to meet their Father-Creator. Oh, what visits those must have been! Now they are fearful and hiding. Their fig leaves failed them; they sensed their nakedness before a Holy God. Knowing they were guilty, they dared not stand trial but fled from justice. Satan promised them they would be as gods—yet here they are as criminals, trembling, anxious to escape, prisoners to sin. For the first time they experienced shame. . . .

Since then until now, we live our days self-consciously. Some are conscious of how well they are doing; others of how poorly they are doing; but all of us are in love with self; looking for a place to hide.

The startling question God spoke forth—**"Where are you?"** 'Where have you gone Adam? Why aren't you with Me?' Adam was God's friend, His chosen creation, His favorite. So much had been done for Adam, but now the Lord must ask, **"Where are you?"**

This question is not to discover what *place*, but what *condition* Adam is now in. This is not the voice of a policeman, but the voice of yearning love. To each of us this call is sounded forth, **"Where are you?"**

One day, God will speak that word to all of those who know not Jesus Christ at the Great White Throne

Judgment of Revelation 20. When He speaks in that day the sea will give up its dead, the graves, death, and hell. All the dead will stand before God because He is going to say, 'Rise.' Every person who has ever sinned will stand before God. There will be no escape.

Those without Christ must seriously consider where they are—in bondage to Satan, separated from God and on the road to ruin. THANK GOD that He went after Adam! The Good Shepherd has now gone after His sheep that are lost. God's first words to fallen man still speak of His grace. It is a question to draw them out of hiding . . . a voice to penetrate his conscience and lead man to conviction over his sin.

This question, **"Where are you?"** proves that man was lost and God had come to seek him. How kind is this God! He comes not to issue the sentence of death, but to preach the gospel. God seeks sinners!

It was not Adam who sought after God, but God that sought after him (Rom. 3:11). What could God have seen in man to cause Him to seek him out? Fallen human beings are precious to God. Hiding from God remains as part of our condition. **"I was afraid."** The prospect of meeting God brought terror. Once secure in his beloved-ness, Adam was never troubled with thoughts of insignificance or failure. Clothed with the sense of Divine worth he was motivated by love, not duty or addictions. So the serpent's goal was reached . . . to separate man from the Image-Maker.

We still are afraid to admit our sin before God and come out of our denial. If Adam had known God's love, he would not have been afraid; for perfect love casts out fear (1 John 4:17,18). God will not only be man's Creator, but He will also become man's Savior! God has come to make HIMSELF our Hiding Place!

"Who told you that you were naked?" Adam KNEW he was naked. This proves that a conscience, a moral instinct, had come to life within him. Our conscience still bears witness to the wicked and desperate condition of man. It is an accuser, tormenting us when we do wrong. Conscience is the still, small voice of the Creator within our heart (1 John 3:19,20). Adam knew he was naked even with fig leaves. This nakedness Adam felt was a moral and spiritual one. Adam, like all of us, laid the blame upon someone else, and indirectly upon God Himself. It seems we will blame someone anything else, before accepting the blame of our own actions. When true conviction grips the heart, we cry out—"It is **I** who has sinned and done evil."

Man has lost all. His dominion, his dignity, his innocence, and his peace with God—all were taken from him. There he stood—a lost, guilty, ruined sinner. Instead of a brokenhearted confession, he tried to excuse himself. The full sense and impact of Adam's reply is more horrible than what appears on the surface.

First, it was not very chivalrous. That was his wife standing there. When he was accused of sin he blamed his wife. On top of that, when he blamed his wife he really abdicated his position as head of the household, saying to God, 'I simply did what the woman told me.' The woman did no better, blaming the serpent. Sin is a brat that no one is willing to own.

Do you think there was ever marital harmony after this? Do you think she ever let him forget it? There is no such indication in the Bible, but I am sure that every time there was a little argument she would say, "Do you remember what you told God? You said it was my fault." This was the beginning of marital disharmony. Only the love of Christ can heal the wounds between men and women.

The Curse of the Fall (3:14-19)

God now turned to the serpent, degrading the shining serpent into a loathsome reptile crawling on his belly, cursed to eat dust. Man was formed from **"dust"** (Gen. 3:19, Isa. 65:25, Mic. 7:17). Every area of our life that is not surrendered to God will become food for the devil. Our uncrucified, stubborn heart becomes the devil's dining room if we do not have a constant "Yes" in our spirit to God. Withholding our life from God feeds the enemy.[3] The only place he can thrive is in the carnal minds of men. Nevertheless, to dust we *do not* have to return. We have been lifted out of dust and seated in the heavens (1 Sam. 2:8, Isa. 52:2, Eph. 2:6).

The **"offspring of the woman"** (Lit.'Seed') is an obvious reference to the Lord Jesus Christ. He is the True Seed of spiritual life that was planted into death, but now springs forth to bear much fruit in His spiritual offspring. Every other human born on earth is from the seed of the man, only Jesus, virgin-born, can be called the seed of the woman. Jesus was *"born of a woman"* (Gal. 4:4). This is a remarkable prophecy of the Virgin Birth of our Lord Jesus (Isa. 7:14).

The True SEED of the woman bound the serpent as the 'stronger man' while He was on earth (Matt. 12:29). Jesus, as the SEED of the woman bound the serpent and plundered all his wealth. In John 14:30, He told His disciples that the serpent ("the prince of the world") had nothing in Him. As the SEED of the woman He crushed the serpent's head on the cross and was raised again in power as the Life-Giving Savior. By woman had come the curse, and by woman would come the Savior. By woman paradise was lost and by the SEED of the woman will regain paradise. She is now dignified and delivered "through childbearing" (1 Tim. 2:15).

Before He banishes them from the garden, He gives them this remarkable promise of a coming Redeemer. In the Hebrew language, the "seed" of the woman is masculine singular. **"HE will crush your head, and you will strike His heel."** This is a clear prophecy of Christ on the Cross! No sooner does man fall into sin than God supplies a revelation of the Cross. On the cross, Satan will strike His heel, but Jesus Christ will crush his head. The cross destroys the works of Satan in the human spirit. Devastation is reversed, and Divine life comes rushing back into the heart. On the cross, the full payment of Adam's transgression was paid and removed by the sacred blood. The serpent's "head" is crushed at the cross. The Goliath of hell has fallen. Nails pierced the flesh of the Son of God, but the blood of the cross was THE FATAL BLOW to Satan (Col. 2:14,15, Heb. 2:14).

The Holy SEED of the woman has overthrown Satan's power as He took our sins on the cross. Satan's wound can never be healed! This perpetual curse on the serpent is also a curse upon the rulers of darkness who roam the earth today. God's eternal curse is upon them; giving the Christian dominion over all of them (Ps. 91:13, Luke 10:19, Eph. 1:19, 23, 1 John 5:18). Redeemed man carries the authority of the cross and resurrection of Jesus

Christ as a weapon of righteousness against the schemes of the enemy. He may bruise us, but we will ultimately, crush him under our feet (Rom. 16:20).

Christ has been sown into us as the SPIRITUAL SEED of the woman. The Parable of the Sower (Matthew 13) teaches us that Christ has sown Himself as the seed into our hearts. The apostle Peter says that we have been born again, not by a corrupting seed, but by an Incorruptible SEED, the living and abiding Word of God (1 Pet. 1:23). Christ is the Living Word, the Incorruptible SEED. The seed of a Conqueror is in you! Every Christian has this SPIRITUAL SEED, which will one day produce the Man-Child, a corporate expression of Jesus in His Church. Look again at the words of one of the stanzas of the great Christmas hymn, "Hark the Herald Angels Sing":

> *Come, Desire of nations, come!*
> *Fix in us Thy humble home:*
> *Rise, the woman's conquering seed,*
> *Bruise in us the serpent's head;*
> *Adam's likeness now efface,*
> *Stamp Thine image in its place:*
> *Final Adam from above,*
> *Reinstate us in Thy love.*

To the woman God speaks His judgment: Motherhood would be accompanied by pain and suffering. It is as though the pain of sin is experienced in the birth of every human being. Because the woman persuaded the man to eat forbidden fruit, she would now find herself in difficult interpersonal relations with him. The battle of the sexes began in the garden. Sin brings grief and competition to their home.

"Cursed is the ground because of you!"

Man was condemned to exhausting labor to make a living. The *ground* was cursed, not Adam or Eve. Because of this curse, the earth would no longer produce food without the laboring toil[4] of man. All of the created earth is subjected to *"frustration,"* waiting for the *"sons of God to be revealed"* (Rom. 8:19,22).

The ground is also a picture of the flesh of man, producing only wood, hay, and straw—striving by works to please God (1 Cor. 3:12,13, Heb. 6:7,8). Plant diseases, droughts, floods, hurricanes and other disasters that would affect food gathering, even food shortages—are all a result of man's disobedience. Before the fall the earth was free of weeds. Thorns and thistles would add to the strife, as Adam's race would eat food by the sweat of his brow. **"Thorns and thistles"** are a sign of man's self-defeat and God's judgment (Prov. 24:31, Isa. 34:13, Num. 33:55). Thorns and thistles are seen as the cares of this life and the deceitfulness of riches (Matt. 13:3-9, 18-23).

Jesus wore the crown of thorns on His head to show that He is taking our curse from us (John 19:2). He sweats great drops of blood while praying in the garden to show us that He is removing our heavy yoke of bondage (Luke 22:44). The curse of God fell on the ground because of Adam's sin. There is a principle here that the sin of a people is absorbed into the land. The land (even nations) carry the curse of the ancestors whose sins fell upon the ground. The blood of Christ is the only thing which can break this curse.

Sorrow . . . Sweat . . . Dust . . . Death . . . The wages of sin. What a fantasy were the serpent's words, **"You shall be like gods!"** As deep and devastating is the fall of man—

so the redeeming grace of God is deeper still! Jesus took our sorrows, sweated great drops of blood, was laid in *"the dust of death"* (Ps. 22:15), as He became a curse for us (Gal. 3:13)! Through our redemption, Jesus not only reversed the effects of the fall, He has brought a better thing. We have gained more through the Last Adam than we lost through the first Adam.

Before the fall, man lived in an earthly paradise, but in Christ, we dwell in the heavenly places (Eph. 2:6). Before the fall we were innocent, in Christ we are made the right-eousness of God, partakers of a Divine Nature (2 Cor. 5:21, 2 Pet. 1:4). Adam was lord over Eden; we are-heirs of all things, *"heirs of God and joint heirs with Christ"* (Rom. 8:17). Jesus is not ashamed to call us brethren (Heb. 2:11). We know the bliss of pardoned sin and union with Christ. Truly, where sin once abounded, grace now much more abounds!

---

[1] It was a fig tree that Jesus cursed for bearing no fruit (Matt. 21:19). The fig tree was the only thing Jesus cursed while on earth. This is a picture of what we hide behind to cover our spiritual shame. It ends up as a curse to us, bearing no fruit.

[2] "The cool of the day" can also be translated, 'the breath of the evening.' The word for 'breath' is taken from the same root word for God's breathing upon Adam. Adam not only walked in a gentle breeze before his fall, he walked in the breath of God, the unhindered Spirit of the Lord . . .

[3] The serpent of Genesis 3 grows into the Dragon of Revelation 12 by feast-ing on the "dust" of fallen humanity.

[4] It is interesting that the Hebrew word for his "toil" is the same Hebrew word for her "pain."

CHAPTER SIX

ADAM'S FAITH &
GOD'S PROVISION

*"The Lord God made garments
of skin . . . and clothed them"*

Note the seven results of the fall of humanity:

1. The ground was cursed—Christ was made a curse for us!

2. Sorrow & tears are a part of our lives—Christ the Man of Sorrows!

3. Sweat is a part of the curse—Christ sweats drops of blood!

4. Thorns and thistles—Christ was given a crown of thorns!

5. Suffering & death entered earth—Jesus suffered & died for us!

6. A Sword kept man from God—By Piercing Christ's side it opened the way to God!

7. Man is separated from God—*"Why have you forsaken me?"*

What faith Adam proved by naming his wife, EVE ('living', or 'life-giver')! She could have been called the mother of all the *dying*. Yet, faith believed the words God had spoken about the SEED of the woman. The prophecy of the cross was received in his heart and he named his wife, Eve, **"the mother of all the living."** By naming her this, Adam sealed this covenant and confirmed the promise of God.

To show that Adam's faith justified him before God, the Creator now provides **"garments"** of animal skins for Adam and his wife. The Lord Himself acted as their priest and provided a sacrifice to cover their sin. God had to strip away this fabricated covering, and presented His own. God took a lamb, hung it on a tree before their eyes, and removed its fleece to clothe this fallen pair! Their first sight of death was an innocent sacrifice, killed for them.

God offered Himself to man as food from the Tree of Life so that man would take Him in, eat Him, and have Him as life. But man refused and fell into sin. God then provided Himself as a Lamb. As Adam rested in the Lamb as his clothing, his covering, he could still live. The first drop of blood seen by man was shed by God, providing salvation for them. By this illustration, God taught Adam and Eve about the Cross. Salvation required a Substitute. Mercy sought to spare the sinner, but justice required an innocent substitute. God taught them what salvation would require, and what it would impart.

The robe God provided was adequate; the fig leaves Adam used were not. So God's righteousness will cover man's sin while man's righteousness is always sin-stained and inadequate (Isa. 28:20, 64:6, Zech. 3:3-5, Luke

15:22,23). When Adam stood clothed with God's garments he could not say he was naked . . . there was no reason to hide from God while wearing the garments of righteousness!

Clothed in lambskin our trembling parents, Adam and Eve, looked like lambs. Although he was a man, Adam had become a lamb in the eyes of God. Since we are covered in Christ, the Lamb of God, and have been given His righteousness (Gal. 3:27) we now express and resemble Him. The sinner becomes one with the Substitute. Even the clothing made for him preached the gospel. One day you will meet Adam and Eve in heaven! It is time for YOU to know the dress you wear. Do YOU possess this seamless ROBE? (See Rev. 3:18, Isa. 61:10.)

Expulsion from Eden (3: 22-24)

Fallen man must not be allowed to eat of the Tree of Life, or he would live forever in his present condition. The Tree of Life must only be tasted in resurrection (Rev. 2:7, 22:2). To live forever in a body of sin and death would be intolerable for God's purpose with man. God wants man to live in Christ, not in his sins (John 5:11,12). He was therefore, driven out of the garden into a world that bore the marks of the curse. God covered their faces with shame so that men would seek Him (Ps. 83:16). He drove man out . . . and kept him out (Job 18:18).

A detachment of cherubim with the flaming sword was left to guard the tree from man. Nevertheless, the Lord Jesus Christ has opened "a new and living way" into the Paradise of God, the Holiest of Holies (Heb. 10:20, John 14:6). Jesus restores Eden and opens the veil for man back into Paradise. The Last Adam was made to leave a garden, so He might bear the sins of the world (Mark 14:46).

This is the first reference to the sword in the Bible. We know from Hebrews 4:12 that the sword is a picture of the Word of God as it judges the intentions of the heart. We still have to pass through the ministry of the **"flaming sword"** to get back into the place where God desires us to dwell. This sword was *"awakened"* against the Lord Jesus Christ as He paid the full price to redeem us to God (Zech. 13:7). Because the Shepherd was smitten, we sheep are spared!

We usually read this passage as though God has barred man from the tree . . . and there is no way to get back in. But that is not true. There is a way to return to this Tree, but it is not a physical way . . . it is through a spiritual Way named Jesus Christ. *"I am the Way, the Truth, and the Life"* were the words of the One who once walked with Adam and Eve in the cool of the day in His Temple-Garden. . . .

The Jamieson, Fausset, and Brown commentary of Genesis translates the last verse of this chapter, *"And He (God) dwelt at the east of the Garden of Eden between the Cherubim, as a Shekinah (a fire-tongue, or fire sword) to keep open the way to the Tree of Life."* The inference here is that God 'tabernacled' at the entrance to the Garden in the flames of the Cherubim—His MERCY SEAT!

Man was not cast out of the garden, but from the glorified presence of God. The triumph of Jesus Christ made it possible for the veil of separation to be torn from top to bottom, providing access to this Mercy Throne. God's desire is that man would enjoy Him as the Tree of

Life, but His glory (the cherubim[1]), His holiness (the slaying sword), and His righteousness (the flaming fire) kept fallen man away. No one can get through these three—the cherubim, the slaying sword, and the flaming fire. If man is ever to eat of the Tree of Life, he must fulfill the requirements of God's glory, holiness, and righteousness.

> The *cherubim* speak of the **Glory of God**
> The *fire* speaks of the **Holiness of God**
> The *sword* speaks of the **Righteousness of God**

Today, we may approach Him as we pass before the flaming Sword of the Word of God held by the cherubim. The images of the cherubim were woven into the veil of the Temple. When the veil was torn apart by God, the cherubim were symbolically moved aside as if God was reopening the eastern gate to the Tree of Life, Jesus Christ. At the cross, man was given free access into the Garden of Eden, through the sinless sacrifice of the Last Adam! Now the flaming sword, once held by the cherubim, is placed inside our heart . . . *"Your Word I have hidden in my heart, that I might not sin against You"* (Ps. 119:11). This flaming sword keeps us safe from the true enemy . . . sin (Heb. 4:12). What are the signs of spiritual death today?

1. We are 'naked,' vulnerable to hurt, accusation & guilt.

2. We hide our true self, an instinctive reaction to guilt.

3. We blame-shift . . . it is someone else's fault.

4. We point our finger at God, blaming Him.

5. Life is difficult, painful, and burdensome; even though we yearn after freedom.

So the Garden of Delight is left . . . Millenniums passed in a moment, a million miles passed in a step. The depths of woe were tasted in a bite, and a hell of suffering experienced in an act. God mistrusted and Satan embraced. Sin's door is flung wide open as the Gate Beautiful to the Garden of God is shut! Man is now emigrating from God and losing the light that once burned bright. With a broken heart and a guilty conscience Adam and Eve begin a different life outside of Eden's gateway. . . .

---

[1] The Guardians of the life and holiness of God (Ex. 26:31-33, Ps. 80:1, 99:1).

CHAPTER SEVEN

AM I MY BROTHER'S KEEPER?

*"On Cain and his offering
He did not look with favor."*

In Chapter Three we saw the beginning of sin *in mankind*, now in Chapter Four we see the beginning of sin *in the family*. Sin is a contaminating leprosy, spreading death in its wake. In Chapter three sin was against God, here it is against man. When we lose the fear of God, we will not respect our fellow man. How devastating is the poison of sin!

Adam and Eve had many sons and daughters (Gen. 5:4), but Cain and Abel seem to have been the two eldest. Some even believe they were twins. Eve said after the birth of her firstborn, Cain, **"With the help of the Lord I have brought forth a man."**

The Hebrew name **"Cain,"** sounds like the Hebrew word for 'brought forth,' or 'acquired.' Many Hebrew scholars believe a more accurate translation would read, 'I have gotten a man–Jehovah' (the God-man).[1] Meaning, Eve believed the promise of her "SEED" (3:15) and thought Cain to be the promised one. What a disappointment when Cain became a murderer!

Imagine the hope and anticipation Adam and Eve had for their firstborn. They had never seen life given that way before. This was the first baby born in the world. It was a marvelous, miraculous experience. Think of all the wonders of childbirth and what happens when we have our first babies. We would have painted the nursery blue. We would have dreamed about all the great things this baby would accomplish. But, instead of being the Christ, he is a killer.

The second son born to Adam and Eve was "**Abel.**" His name means 'vanity' or 'fading away.' Perhaps this is because their hope for the Messiah had faded. Or maybe they saw from the thorns and thistles and hard ground that life was much more difficult outside the Garden than inside, and their joy faded away. Paul tells us in Romans 8 that the world was made subject to vanity. Adam and Eve saw this 'vanity' firsthand and named their son, Abel . . .

Cain was a farmer and Abel was a shepherd. Both men were fulfilling God's command to subdue the earth. Since he was a farmer, Cain offered the fruit of the ground. In bringing the offering made of the product of the cursed earth, Cain was denying that he was a guilty sinner. He insisted on approaching God based on personal worthiness.

Abel was a shepherd. Sheep were not used for food prior to the flood (Gen. 1:29), but for <u>sacrifice</u>. Abel had his heart set on the coming Sacrifice. He confessed his sin and brought the first and best of his flock as a sacrifice in faith. Abel acknowledged he was worthy of death and that God required a substitute. Abel presented his offering *"by faith"* (Heb. 11:4)

Cain and Abel brought their offering **"unto the Lord."** There was apparently a specific place where they were supposed to go. In verse 16 we read, *"And Cain went out from the presence of the Lord."* That seems to indicate there was a specific place where God dwelt. It could very well be that the Shekinah glory was suspended there over a mercy seat where the cherubim stood guard and where they would go at various times to offer their sacrifices.

"The Lord looked with favor on Abel and his offering, but on Cain and his offering he did not look with favor." The attitude of Abel's heart was right, making his sacrifice acceptable. Cain's heart was not right, and thus he brought a polluted offering. Worship is a matter of the heart. God did not just care about the correct offering, but the attitude of the heart. God detests the sacrifice of the wicked (Prov. 15:8). Cain's bloodless offering was not accepted for he could not face his sin. Sin's guilt must be removed.

You can almost see the fruit Cain brought . . . a big fruit buffet. How beautiful with its pineapples and apples and figs and other delightful fruits! It is certainly more colorful than a meat buffet. When you look at a bloody pot roast compared to oranges and bananas and apples and grapes, there is no comparison. Cain brought a tremendous offering of the most beautiful fruit imaginable. But it was without the shedding of blood and could never cleanse sin's stain.

It was not that God did not want the fruit. Later on, in Leviticus 19:24, God will say, 'Bring the fruit.' The problem is that Cain had it out of sequence. Before we can bring the fruit we must have forgiveness and new life. First, the blood that brings the forgiveness of sins then the fruit of praise and good works. Cain had it out of order. He wanted to bring the praise without forgiveness. So God had no respect for Cain's offering. He did have respect for Abel's offering. Abel's bloodstained sacrifice signified:

1. He believed the report of his parents. God had killed a lamb and covered them with its skin.

2. His sin required the death of an innocent one to cover his guilt before God. Abel, by faith, knew that God could be approached through a sacrifice.[2] This is why in Matthew 23:35 he is called "righteous Abel." The tree must be good or the fruit cannot be pleasing to the heart-searching God.

Cain and Abel take us back to the *true* worship of God and the *false* worship of God. Here we have traced back to their fountainhead the two streams that empty themselves in Heaven and in Hell. They are the saved and the lost . . . and the dividing line between them in a line of blood.

Abel is a clear type of Jesus Christ who, as a Shepherd, brought the sacrifice of Himself to God and was killed by His jealous brethren (John 15:25, Matt. 27:18). Abel's offering is called by God, *"a better sacrifice"*(Heb. 11:4) and he was therefore *"commended as a righteous man."* Cain thought of himself just as acceptable as Abel. Abel was not better, his sacrifice was.

It is possible that a regular worship system had been established. The text indicates there was an *appointed time* to bring the sacrifices. We must assume that they had been going on a regular basis making offerings to the Lord.

Since Cain was a tiller of the ground and Abel was a tender of sheep, it is likely they had already offered blood sacrifices to God at the gateway to Eden. Cain would have had to purchase his from his younger brother Abel. As the months and years wore on Cain began to chafe under the need to continually go to his brother for a sacrifice . . . Cain began to rebel. His pride began to well up and it became too much for him. He had lost faith. He was the number one son and through him the blessings were supposed to come. Now he had lost that right. He had lost faith.

Every time Cain bought a lamb from Abel, he would hear from Abel, "Isn't this great that God gives us a way to cleanse our sin and to go into His presence?" Cain would chafe under that because he was of the evil one. As the months and years went on, he began to hate this method that God had prescribed. He began to rebel as his father Adam had. He rebelled against God's prescribed method for coming into His presence.

When Cain brought his offering, he fully expected the fire of God to fall and consume it in a mushroom cloud, and for his brother Abel, nothing. That is not what happened at all. God had no regard for Cain's offering, but fire fell on Abel's offering.

As Cain saw himself passed over while his brother was blessed, his heart was filled with rage. Cain was furious that all of his labors counted for nothing. He rejected the Lord's counsel and became angry over his brother's approved sacrifice. If Cain's offering had been presented in the right spirit, there would not have been anger in his heart when he realized God had not accepted it. Instead, he would have had a humble, teachable heart to learn the ways of God.

Cain never asked God, "What is wrong? Lord, what can I change?" He was merely angry and jealous. Cain turned away from presenting a blood sacrifice, and turned instead to his own reason and vain conceit. Professing himself to be wise, he became a fool (Rom. 1:22). God had ordained the way to approach Him, but Cain chooses the way of self-will.

"If you do what is right will you not be accepted?" God is speaking about offering the RIGHT sacrifice (a blood sacrifice, not the fruit of the cursed earth). The Hebrew literally says, *'Will you not have the excellency?'* or *'Will you not be exalted?'* This refers to the rights and privileges of the firstborn. For only by bringing an acceptable sacrifice would he qualify to rule over his brother.

As Cain saw his brother's sacrifice accepted, he reasoned that his little brother would now be the ruler over him. This is what angered him the most. He decided he would rather kill his brother than to be ruled by him. This is the real motive and the cause of the first murder in history . . . jealousy! Brother Cain just could not stand the thought of someone being blessed over him!

Jealousy and violence are an issue of worship. Cain wanted to worship God his own way. He became angry when he could not. So many today insist on bringing to the Lord the worship THEY believe is right, instead of what God truly desires. So the Lord was giving Cain the opportunity to humble himself and be glad over his brother's accepted sacrifice. In doing this it would bring exaltation, teaching him how to rule over sin. If Cain had been glad in his heart that his brother's sacrifice was respected, he would have gained what all of us are looking for: elevation, exaltation and dignity. He was being offered a chance to be exalted by God.

This is not only the way to be elevated and honored; it is the way to rule over sin. If we can rejoice over others being honored even above us . . . when our offering is inferior to theirs, we have learned how to rule over sin.

God was clearly telling Cain that if he would offer the right sacrifice he could regain the rights of the firstborn. The real difference between Cain and Abel was in their sacrifice, for even Cain would be cleansed if he did (*offered*) what is right.

However, at the same time, God solemnly warned him of a greater sin **"crouching"** outside, desiring to have him. The word used here is a word picture of sin, like a lion, crouching in the shadows to maul him. The Hebrew word for door is literally 'opening' (i.e. the door of his conscience, the opening of his soul).

The first edition of the Jewish Publication Society's *Torah* offered this translation; 'Sin is the demon at the door.' His sin would spring up like a beast and devour him! The serpent talked Eve into her sin, but not even God could talk Cain out of his. God told Cain, **"You must master it (sin)."**

Sin is always the fault of man. We do not sin accidentally. God tells us that we have the responsibility to master sin. How do we master sin? By offering a faith sacrifice . . . trusting in the blood of the innocent substitute—The Lamb of God. His Cross is the key to victory over sin. He is the Master, who mastered sin, by his sinless life, and his sacrificial death. We master sin when we yield to the Life of the Master . . . the One who mastered sin in every dimension.

The First Murder (4:8–16)

"Now Cain said to his brother . . ." The verb "said" has an unusual use here. It is a rare Hebrew word used only in some of the old cognate languages. It is used in other ancient literature to mean, 'making an arrangement for a meeting.' If that is the translation here, then it is saying that Cain made arrangements for a meeting with Abel. So whatever Cain is going to do, it is premeditated. He is making arrangements for a meeting out in the field, far from any possible interference. He already knows what he is going to do. It is first-degree, premeditated murder.

As they walked toward this remote area, Abel, whom the New Testament calls a prophet, was probably exhorting and encouraging his brother in regard to what God had said to him. "Cain, you need to submit yourself to God and get rid of that prideful spirit. Go back. I will sell you a lamb; I will give you a lamb. Offer it to God and He will be satisfied and accept you." So, as Abel is preaching to him in the field, he slays him. . . .

The very first death in the Bible was the death of a martyr who died because of his faith. Cain's act of murder was the devastating consequence of false worship and religious jealousy. In 1 John 3:12 we learn that *"Cain . . . belonged to the evil one."* Why did he murder his own brother? *"Because his own actions were evil and his brother's were righteous."* There is nothing worse than religious jealousy. This is what caused the death of our Lord Jesus Christ. The religious system could not understand how Jesus could be approved of God over them.

O, the darkness of sin—Cain killed his own brother, a good brother who had done nothing wrong. In killing his brother, Cain was striking out at God, for it was God's acceptance of Abel that gave birth to the envy filling his heart. Cain hated him, because God loved him. Yet how many times do we speak evil or hold malice in our hearts toward one of our own brethren in Christ? To hate a brother is the sin that Cain committed (Matt. 5:21, 22, 1 John 3:15).

On the way back from the murder scene, God stopped Cain in his tracks asking, **"Where is your brother Abel?"** His self-centered reply was, **"I don't know. Am I my brother's keeper?"** This is a statement of sarcasm, for it could rightly be translated, 'I don't know. Shall I shepherd the shepherd!'[3] Cain rejected responsibility for his sin. God gave Cain a chance to repent by asking, **"Where is your brother Abel?"**

The Creator sought to draw out a confession, but Cain pleads not guilty, adding rebellion to his sin. He covered a deliberate murder with a deliberate lie; **"I don't know."** But how can one hide sin from God? Cain was insolent, blurting out, **"Am I my brother's keeper?"** NOT, 'Am I my brother's murderer?'

We speak the language of Cain when we neglect to show concern for the hungry, the destitute, the broken, and the defenseless (Phil. 2:4). Although everyone is responsible for his or her own actions, we cannot turn away from one in need (1 John 3:17,18). Innocent blood cried out for justice from the ground. God speaks as if Abel's blood were both witness and prosecutor. The most important words in this sentence are **"TO ME"**—the blood cries out to God and He hears it. Blood has a voice!

---

[1] It was four thousand years later when the Virgin Mary gave birth to a child whose name Jesus means, 'Jehovah, the Savior.'

[2] How do we know that God accepted Abel's sacrifice? Perhaps fire fell from heaven as a sign! Lev. 9:24, Jude 6:21, 1 Kings 18:38, 1 Chron. 21:26

[3] The word keeper is literally 'shepherd.' Cain was saying to God, "Am I my brother's shepherd? Abel is the shepherd, not me. Don't ask me where he is." His reply was most arrogant.

CHAPTER EIGHT

THE CRY OF BLOOD

The Lord said . . . 'Blood cries out to Me!'

Blood crying is a symbol of the soul crying out for the right to live, and a demand for the punishment of the murderer. Bloodguilt calls for justice even from the ground. It is as if the face of the earth blushes as it becomes stained by blood. The Hebrew word is in the plural, 'Your brother's *BLOODS* . . .' This speaks of his descendants that could have lived—their blood too, cries out against Cain. The blood of Abel cries out for vengeance. But the blood of Christ cries out for mercy and pardon. This is why the blood of Christ speaks a better word than the blood of Abel (Heb. 12:24). Abel is a type or picture of Jesus Christ:

♦ Abel was a shepherd. The Lord Jesus is the Good Shepherd (John 10), the Chief Shepherd (1 Pet. 5:4) and the great Shepherd (Heb. 13:20). *"The Lord is my shepherd"* (Ps. 23:1).

♦ Abel was hated by his brother without a cause. We read in John 15:25 that Jesus was hated by His brethren.

+ Abel was slain because of envy. Cain was envious because his brother found acceptance in the sight of God and he did not. Matthew 27:18 says that the Lord Jesus was delivered up because of envy.

+ Abel did not die a natural death, but a violent death at wicked hands. Acts 2:23 says Jesus died by wicked hands.

+ Abel was slain by his brother according to the flesh . . . and so was Jesus Christ (Acts 2:36).

+ The blood of Abel still speaks (Heb. 11:4); the blood of Jesus still speaks (Heb. 12:24).

Sustenance and shelter were both taken from Cain. As a wanderer he would spend his days with a stained and condemning conscience. He would remain a fugitive and a vagabond all the days of his life as he carried the **"mark of Cain."**

This mark would be both a mark of rejection and a mark of protection. Cain is cursed, separated to evil and under the wrath of God. We have all deserved this curse, and it is only in the grace of Christ that we inherit a blessing instead (Gal. 3:10,13). Every fallen human being carries the mark of Cain—*rejection*.

Every one of Cain's race knows that deep inside they are not acceptable. Fear of rejection and the fear of man are the fruits of sin. Fear brings insecurity; leaving us all with facades of independence and self-sufficiency to protect us from rejection. Only the Blood of Christ and the love of our Bridegroom-King can remove these fears from the heart. In His love we become secure.

Cain complained of the sentence passed upon him. He does not acknowledge the greatness of his sin, only the greatness of his punishment (Lam. 3:39). He sees himself exposed to the hatred and ill will of all mankind. Wherever he wanders, he will be in danger of his life. Unpardoned guilt fills the heart of man with unspeakable terrors (Prov. 28:1, Job 15:20-35, Ps. 53:4,5).

God decrees, **"If anyone kills Cain, he will suffer vengeance seven times over."** If Cain had been killed immediately, he would have been forgotten. By preserving his life, God makes Cain a monument of justice. With the mark[1] of Cain, he would be distinguished forever as the man who killed his brother. Cain is then banished from the presence of the Lord to the land of Nod ('wandering'). Cain renounced God, leaving the presence of the Lord to a life of futile wandering . . . *"way of Cain"* (Jude 11).

The Way of Cain

Notice what the Bible says about *"the way of Cain:"*

1. The way of human reason.
2. The way of unconfessed sin.
3. The way of jealousy.
4. The way of anger and strife with a brother.
5. The way of self-righteousness striving to please God.
6. The way of murder.
7. The way of condemnation.
8. The way of despair.
9. The way of wandering.

The Descendants of Cain (4:17-24)

This early civilization, which perished in the judgment of the flood was somewhat advanced. Cities were built, along with the development of the arts and manufacturing. They deliberately excluded God from their thoughts (Rom. 1:18-23). The descendants of Cain took the lead in producing cities, music, weapons, and agricultural implements . . . civilization itself. This is the way of the world as humanity copes with life under the curse of sin (Psalm 17:14, 127:1). Man produces a culture without God.

God sentenced Cain to wandering. Capital punishment is a lesson of justice that God will teach man after the flood, but for now, Cain receives a life sentence . . . Out of rebellion he now builds a city, to permanently locate in defiance to the Most High. . . .

It *is* God's intention for mankind to live in a city. This is the dream of God, a city called the New Jerusalem and a people called the Bride of Christ. This bridal-city will one day be the dwelling place of both God and men; the city whose Builder and Architect is God. It will not come until man is ready to live within it. In our arrogance we go about building cities without God, assuming we are able to live together without the grace and presence of Christ. Our imposing cities and technical brilliance are dim shadows compared to the light of the coming city shining bright as the sun. . . .

The family of the fugitive is formed. Cain, of necessity, married one of his sisters (Gen. 5:4) who gave birth to Enoch. By naming the city after his son, Enoch, Cain was attempting to retain the memory of his descendants (Ps. 49:10,11).

The line of Cain continues with Enoch, Irad, Mehujael, Methushael, and Lamech.

The Line of Cain	The Line of Seth
Adam	Adam
Cain	Seth
Enoch	Enosh
Irad	Kenan
Mehujael	Mahalalel
Methushael	Jared
Lamech	Enoch
Jabal	Methuselah
Jubal	Lamech
Tubal-Cain	Noah
Naamah	Shem
	Ham
	Japheth

Now let's look at the meaning of the names of the line of **CAIN**:

Adam	=	man
Cain	=	selfishness
Enoch	=	teaches
Irad	=	fugitive
Mehujael	=	blotted out by God, God is combating
Methusael	=	they died who are of God
Lamech	=	overcomer, powerful, one who brings low

Here is what the names of the descendants of Cain show us:

MAN is SELFISH and this TEACHES us that when we become a FUGITIVE from His presence, GOD will COMBAT us until we are BLOTTED OUT BY GOD in judgment. Many good people are persecuted, and THEY DIED WHO ARE OF GOD even when evil men are POWERFUL and seek to be OVERCOMERS, God will BRING THEM LOW! Notice the meaning of the names of Seth's line:

Adam	=	man
Seth	=	appointed
Enosh	=	pain or suffering
Kenan	=	to die
Mahalalel	=	the splendor of God
Jared	=	come down
Enoch	=	teaches, instructs
Methuselah	=	his death will bring
Lamech	=	powerful, overthrower
Noah	=	rest

The descendants of Seth show that MAN is APPOINTED to PAIN and SUFFERING, and TO DIE. But the SPLENDOR OF GOD, Jesus Christ, has COME DOWN to TEACH us how HIS DEATH WILL BRING into our lives the POWERFUL OVERCOMER who will lead us all into REST! What a message hidden in the genealogies!

Lamech was a bloody and barbarous man who took two wives (corrupting God's ideal of marriage as stated in the Garden) and became a man of violence and vengeance. The names of his wives were **Adah** ('adorned'), and **Zillah** ('shadow'). His second wife is only a shadow of a wife, for whenever we turn from the righteous plan of God we take to ourselves only a shadow. The sons of Lamech and Adah were **Jabal** ('nomad' - a man who raised livestock, which suggests wealth), and **Jubal** ('musician' or 'jubilee').

The children of Lamech and Zillah were, **Tubal-Cain** ('a smith or metallurgist' - the inventor of weaponry), and a daughter **Naamah** ('the lovely one'). These became the wealthy, the artisans, and the musicians . . . the beautiful people of their day who walked in the vain spirit of the world. Man has produced a culture without God.

The chorus of Lamech was a threat and warning. He is the ultimate warrior. He has used those instruments of iron made by his son Tubal-Cain. He struts in front of his wives: **"Hear my voice; ye wives of Lamech, hearken unto my speech; for I have slain a man to my wounding, and a young man to my hurt. If Cain shall be avenged sevenfold, truly Lamech seventy and sevenfold."**

The Hebrew text can properly be translated, 'I will kill a man for wounding me, even a youth if he injures me!' This is a violent, angry taunt to others, to leave him alone. He is adding to the sin of Cain with this vow of violence and is not afraid to take even a greater curse than that of Cain.

Do you see the progression here? God told Cain that anyone who injured him would receive sevenfold retribution (4:15). This is what Lamech is referring to. He is saying, 'If God would avenge Cain sevenfold, then I am the type of person who will avenge seventy-seven fold.'[2] Lamech is boastful, arrogant, and an angry reviler of men. We see him telling his wives that killing others will be his business. With a seared conscience he becomes the world's first terrorist.

The Birth of Seth (4:25,26)

Eve gave birth to another son who was prophetically named Seth. Seth means *'appointed'* or *'new beginning.'* Apparently, Adam and Eve realized that this son would be appointed to replace Abel and follow on in the ways of God. This was an act of faith for Adam and Eve. In this child their hopes were renewed. Seth was given a son whom he named Enosh ('mortal' or 'frail'). After the birth of Seth and Enosh, **"men began to call on the Name of the LORD."** Seth realized that human life was weak, frail, and mortal. This is the commencement of corporate worship.

The word, *LORD*, is "Jehovah," which again is the name of the personal God—Covenant Keeper, the God that can be known. The Hebrew states, 'Men began to call on the Name; JEHOVAH.' Worship among men was birthed at this time. This was the first revival/awakening in the Bible! Calling on the name of the Lord implies prayer, worship, and intercession. They stirred themselves to seek God . . . Not only in private, but also in public assemblies.

It is the *Name* of the Lord, the revelation of who He is which draws the heart of every human being to worship. His Name is the true center of spiritual fellowship and intimacy. This worship was maintained and encouraged by Divine revelations from Jehovah; for wherever two or more are gathered in His Name, He will be in their midst. It is always the heart of God to meet with His worshipping people with manifestations of His presence.

We know that prophetic ministry began with the prophecies given by Enoch (Jude 14,15). The prophet

Enoch foretold of the Second Coming of Jesus Christ! God told Adam and Eve about the first coming (Gen. 3:15,21). Enoch, the seventh from Adam, received even more revelation as he prophesied of the return of Christ.

Enoch also prophesied about the flood by naming his son Methuselah. The name Methuselah means, 'his death will bring (i.e. the Flood).' It was the year Methuselah died that the flood came. Do you see why Methuselah lived so long? God was giving mercy to the sons of Adam to repent!

From a single pair in Eden, within seven generations, the human family would have attained to very considerable dimensions. At the birth of Seth, Adam was 130 years old (Gen. 5:3) and had many sons and daughters whose names are not listed (Gen. 5:4). In addition, Cain's posterity would be great enough to populate cities over time between the creation and the Flood. Some have estimated that the population of the earth at the time of Lamech was around 1 million. Civilization without God is chaos . . . chaos as great as Genesis chapter 1.

---

[1] Ancient rabbis taught that the mark of Cain was a horn that grew on his head.

[2] Amazingly, our Lord Jesus told us to forgive seventy times seven; the same phrase Lamech uses here (Matt. 18:21,22). Grace is greater than sin.

CHAPTER NINE

ENOCH

"Enoch walked with God."

Genesis 5 is a remarkable chapter. It is the **"written account of Adam's line."** The history of man begins with death and pain, but will one day end with delight and pleasure, as the redeemed become the dwelling place of God. The destiny of God's people is to become the "New Jerusalem" company who will live forever at His side.

God created male and female and then blessed them. Throughout Genesis, God is the One who loves to bless His people. He called this newly created couple, **"man"**[1] or ADAM. No stronger statement could be made that male and female are coequal before their creator.

There is really only one man in the Old Testament, and that is Adam. There is really only one Man in the New Testament, and that is Jesus. There are really only two men who have represented the human race—the first Adam and the Last Adam, Jesus Christ. The books of Genesis and Matthew both are introduced with the record of the generations of Adam and Christ. . . .

Genesis chapter 5 is a description of the reign of death that came into the human family by sin. It is the 'résumé of death' of the human race. It is filled with names that are difficult to pronounce, with the number of years each one lived; with the repeated words, ". . . and then he died." Death has passed upon all men (Rom. 5:12).

We were originally created in the likeness of God, but Adam's descendants are born **"in his own likeness."** The poison of sin is passed to all generations. His moral likeness was passed to his offspring. Seth was begotten in the likeness of a sinful father. Nothing that man does could change this death sentence. Man is lost and helpless because of sin. The works of man cannot shake off this dominion of death.

Notice that they all lived over eight hundred years, some over nine hundred years. God prolonged their lives to show His mercy and to speedily populate the earth. Many of these listed were able to meet with Adam and hear his own account of the fall, the promise of a Redeemer, the coats of skins being provided, being cast out of the garden.

An interesting comparison can be made of Genesis chapter 5 and Matthew chapter 1. Genesis is the book of death; Matthew is the Lamb's Book of Life. The entire Bible centers on these two books: the book of the generations of Adam, and the book of the generations of Jesus Christ.

Enoch and Methuselah (5:21-27)

The story of Enoch[2] is fascinating. He was born 622 years after Adam was created and heard Adam tell him the stories of God walking in the garden and speaking with them in the cool of the day. Perhaps Enoch's desire for intimacy came from hearing these incredible accounts.

Enoch was the one taught of the Lord as he walked in the Spirit. Here are some of the things we can learn about Enoch's life:

Enoch is a remarkable man of faith and righteousness. He is one of but two men who walked with God and went to heaven without passing through the gates of death. He was a man who pleased God (Heb. 11:5). The days in which he lived were wicked and godless. The corruption of man was filling the earth; he alone seems to have stood faithful in a prophetic ministry. Enoch walked with God in friendship and fellowship. He was a man of faith and purity, for God does not walk with those who hide their sin (1 John 1:6-10). A holy God walked with a sinful man—what grace! To walk with God means we cease walking in our own ways to follow His. It implies a surrendered will (Amos 3:3) with no controversy between them . . . A steady walk with God for hundreds of years! How did Enoch please God? Hebrews 11:5,6 supplies the answer: Enoch was a man of faith.

Enoch walked with God. To walk together with someone means you must like them. Enoch liked God. He enjoyed the sweet communion of walking in the sacred garden with God. They communed one with the other. They enjoyed one another. Enoch loved to be in the presence of God.

As God's friend, he grew in the prophetic anointing and in friendship with the Creator. Enoch's walk with God was not a monastic life full of isolated piety. He was a happily married man with sons and daughters. He did not hide away in a cubicle to please God. He walked with God while living a normal family life. For three hundred years they walked as Divine Friends. Finally, God said . . .

"Enoch, you have walked with Me long enough. Let Me take you to Myself. Instead of going back home to your house tonight, how about just coming home to My house."

Enoch was a prophet. Instructed by the Holy Spirit he walked in the spirit of wisdom and revelation (Eph. 1:16,17). He walked with God in prophetic lifestyle, in sanctified character and spiritual communion. He prophesied about the return of Jesus Christ, thousands of years before Christ was even born. Enoch is the first prophet mentioned in the Bible (Jude 14,15). As a preacher of righteousness he predicted the judgment of the Lord. Many of his spiritual experiences were recorded in the three "Books of Enoch."[3] His writings were respected by many of the early church fathers. He writes of such subjects as angels, which he refers to as "watchers." One of the passages he wrote is quoted in Jude 14,15. It describes him exhorting the people of his day to reform their evil ways.

Enoch was taken away. By faith he was caught up into heaven without seeing death. Enoch was the exception to the rule of death. After reading six times, **"and then he died,"** the seventh time we read, **"God took him away."** Because he did not live like the rest, he did not die like the rest. God took him because He delighted in him. He lived a year for each day of the year—365. God took him as an example of a man who had fulfilled his destiny. God carried him across to the other side. He was walking with God one moment on earth and the next in heaven! Faith had turned to sight, faith turned into perfect fellowship (Rev. 3:4).

There must have been a tremendous manhunt for Enoch. Relatives must have said, "Why did God take him?" Enoch's wife would have asked, "Why?" God took Enoch to be with Himself to show that death was not the end; there is a better place to go. Both Enoch and Elijah did not face death. Elijah was taken up into heaven by a whirlwind. Perhaps the whirlwind of Ezekiel was the escalator that took Enoch into the presence of God.

The Hebrew for, "God took him away" is the word used for someone taking a bride. Enoch's rapture is a picture of the Rapture of the Church, the Bride of Christ. God had made a promise to Enoch that he would never die. By **faith**, he was translated that he should not see death. He believed that he would not see death, and his faith achieved this translation into heaven without dying. His disappearance would have made quite a stir upon society.

There was another Enoch mentioned here in Genesis—Enoch, a son of Cain (Gen. 4:17). The first city in the Bible was named after this Enoch. Not too many of us have a city built in our name! These two Enochs were contemporaries. No doubt, Enoch, the son of Cain was voted more likely to succeed in the eyes of the world. He would be the one that others were sure would be remembered. However, it was Enoch, the son of Jared, who goes down in history as the one, who walked with God so closely, that he disappeared into the glory realm. Which is more important to you, to have a city named after you—or to walk with God?

The son of Enoch was named Methuselah—*'his death will bring.'* This implies that Enoch had a revelation given to him about the judgment of the Flood. God revealed to him that after his son died, the Flood would come. By faith Enoch acted on this revelation and named him, *'his death will bring.'*

Methuselah's life was a statement that the world will last as long as he lives and no longer! It was the very year of Methuselah's death that the Deluge came. No doubt, this is why the long-suffering of the Lord allowed him to live 969 years; the longest living man in the Bible! For 969 years the world was warned about coming judgment! We have been warned even longer than that, for we have had the New Testament for two thousand years. How shall we escape if we neglect the coming judgment of God?

Jewish writers say that Methuselah, Noah's grandfather, died seven days before the flood and that Noah and his family entered the Ark the day Methuselah died (Gen. 7:10). Methuselah's life overlapped Adam's by 243 years.

Noah (5:28-32)

Noah, the great-grandson of Enoch, had a word of prophecy over him when he was born. His father, Lamech, prophesied—**"He will comfort us."** Lamech was obviously a man of faith that believed God's promise and warning through the prophet Enoch. Life under the curse was difficult and toilsome. But God had a plan for Noah . . .

The Hebrew name Noah means *rest*; and it sounds like the Hebrew word *"comfort."* This prophecy was that Noah would become a type of Christ in his building of an Ark and in giving comfort to the human race. The fulfillment of this prophecy would be comfort in the midst of the cursed earth. Noah brought comfort, but the One

Noah typifies, brings us true rest. *"Come unto Me all who are weary and heavy laden, and I will give you REST."*

There is a sense in which Noah becomes the second father of the human race. Noah and his sons repopulated the earth after the Flood. The names of his sons were Shem, Ham, and Japheth. Shem was the father of the Semitic (Abrahamic/Jewish people). Shem means 'fame.' It is the line of Shem from which Jesus was born. Ham was the father of the dark races whose descendants inhabited the torrid regions. His name means 'hot' or 'dark.' Japheth was the father of the Caucasian races. His name means 'spreading forth.'

The "Nephilim"

The following section has been the subject of debate for centuries. Many scholars consider it to be the most difficult passage in Genesis to interpret. The question raised is, who are the **"sons of God"** in verse 2? Are they angels or the godly line of Seth that intermingled with the Canaanite women? Most of the early church fathers interpreted "sons of God" to mean angels that fell from heaven and had sexual relations with the daughters of men (Job 1:6, 38:7). The Syriac version and the Septuagint, (a Greek translation of the Hebrew) reads, 'the angels of God.' A puzzling scenario is presented. Fallen angels having sex with women?

These fallen angels are mentioned in Jude 6 as those who *"did not keep their positions of authority but abandoned their own home."* They are kept in darkness, *"bound with everlasting chains for judgment on the great Day."* In 2 Peter 2:4,5 these fallen angels are spoken of in the context of God's judgment of the world in the days of Noah. The activity of these demonic powers with the daughters of men grieved God's heart and moved Him to destroy the world. Satan was seeking to corrupt the "SEED of the woman" that would come forth to crush him and bruise his head (Gen. 3:15). Satan sought to destroy the human race by producing a race of monstrosities.

This unlawful alliance of demons with women caused the flood. Just like the days of Noah, so shall it be at the coming of the Lord Jesus (Matt. 24:36-42). Demonic offspring will again be brought to birth in the last days. Perhaps the Antichrist will be one of these Nephilim,[4] or 'men of renown.' The "Nephilim" (verse 4) were monsters of iniquity; superhuman beings that were the result of demonic insemination of women.

The warning God gives man is that He will have an end of His patience. His Spirit will not always contend against the perversity of the human heart (Gen. 6:3). The word **"contend"** in Hebrew means 'made low.' God warns, 'My Spirit will not always be made low in man,' or 'My Spirit, the Divine breath, shall not be put low in man forever.'

There is a point we may reach when God will withdraw His hand and give us over to darkness (Rom. 1:18-32). The Spirit of the Lord, provoked by resistance, will not always strive with us. We have the choice to do right or to do evil. If we choose to do what is evil, we will quench the Holy Spirit and shut off His gracious influence upon our life (Hosea 4:17). The Blessed Spirit strives with sinners, convicting the heart and conscience to turn us from sin to God. If we vex the Spirit of God we become ripe for ruin.[5]

God says of man, **"He is mortal"** or 'flesh.' When God created man He became a living soul . . . but now God calls man 'flesh.' The lower life has conquered mankind. As mortals, we will all die (Heb. 9:27). We are frail, short-lived creatures. Because of increased wickedness, God shortened the life span of man from almost a millennium to 120 years.

The time of God's patience with man's sin is sometimes long, but always limited. Reprieves are not pardons. Though God will bear with us for a great while, His patience has an end. God saw the wickedness of man increase and was grieved. When God saw all that He made in Genesis 1-2, He said, *"It is good."* Here God says, **"I am grieved that I have made them!"** Man's wickedness is great in the eyes of a Holy God. It was a stench in His nostrils; it filled His heart with pain and grief beyond our understanding.

Man was created to be in fellowship with his Creator. Now we see man deserting his best Friend to slide even deeper into darkness. Sin provokes God; it grieves His holiness, challenging the Maker to judge mankind (Isa. 63:10).

God saw the fountain of sin in the human heart. Every inclination, every motivation in the heart of man was toward evil continually. There is only rottenness and filth within the heart of man made in His image. How offensive is our sin to God! What a corrupt spring inside each of us! All the violence, oppression, perversity, and corruption cried out to God to judge us. Deceitful and desperately wicked, humanity was plunged even further into sin's dark dungeon (Jer. 17:9). The iniquity of man is a widespread, firmly rooted, deeply staining corruption.

"Every inclination of the thoughts of his heart was only evil all the time." Man dwells in darkness, loving darkness, rather than light, for his deeds are evil (John 3:19-21).

We must take note of the mercy of God shown to the civilization before the Flood:

+ **A gospel of mercy** was given to them in the promise of the SEED of the woman (Gen. 3:15).

+ **A ministry of mercy** was given through the prophesying of Enoch and preaching of Noah.

+ **The Spirit of mercy** was striving with their hearts to turn them to righteousness (Gen. 6:3).

+ **God's grace** was granted in prolonging their days for centuries before the Flood.

If a soul is lost, it is in spite of many mercies. The heart of God was **"filled with pain."** What does it do to you to know that God's heart is filled with pain when we sin against Him? Sin damages a relationship with One who loves us. We violate trust, we ignore His love, and we trample on His grace each time we sin. God does not merely see our sin as a distant judge, but as an offended friend (Isa. 43:24, Ezek. 6:9). Sin wounds Him. Do you want to continue wounding the heart of God?

God's grief was so great that He vowed to destroy all people and all the living creatures of the earth. Sin's judgment would be great and severe . . . The Creator resolves to destroy humanity (Isa. 27:11). The Image-Maker must begin again. . . .

The Hebrew word is 'Adam'—humankind.

[2] Enoch's name means 'dedicated, instructed or experienced.'

[3] The "Book of Jubilees" relates that he was carried into paradise, where he writes down the judgment of all men. Ancient Arabic legend declares him to be the inventor of arithmetic and writing.

[4] Nephilim means, 'giants', or 'mighty ones.'

[5] It is supposed by some scholars that Genesis 6:3 is a quotation from one of Enoch's prophecies contained in the Book of Enoch (Jude 14,15).

"Now the earth was corrupt in God's
sight and was full of violence.
God saw how corrupt the earth
had become, for all the people on earth
had corrupted their ways."

Genesis 6:11,12

CHAPTER TEN

NOAH'S ARK

"But Noah found favor in the eyes of the Lord"

Noah is the first man to be born after Adam dies . . . He sought out the grace of God and laid hold of it. Grace is the foundation of every life that pleases God. It was the GRACE of God, not the virtue of Noah that preserved him from the devastation of judgment. This is the first mention of GRACE in the Bible. It is interesting that it is seen in context of the sin of man at its climax. This clearly shows us that there is nothing within man that would merit the GRACE of God.

It was GRACE that preserved Noah in days of incredible wickedness, enabling him to set his face against the whole current of public opinion and conduct. Yet notice Noah's response to this grace shown to him:

♦ *"Thus did Noah; according to all God commanded him"* (6:22).

♦ *"And Noah did . . . all that the Lord commanded him"* (7:5).

♦ *"There went in two and two unto Noah into the Ark, the male and female, as God had commanded Noah"* (7:9).

♦ *"And they that went in, male and female of all flesh, as
God had commanded him"* (7:16).

Thus four times we are told that Noah did all that
God commanded him. Grace leads to obedience, not
independence or waywardness (Phil. 2:12,13). He was a
solitary and lonely figure because he was the only one
who found favor with God in that terrible, terrible time.
The Scripture says he was a righteous man, blameless in
his generation.

Noah was the tenth from Adam. Ten is the number
of God's expectations of man and man's responsibility to
God (Ten Commandments). God now comes to destroy
the earth. God provides grace to escape the judgment—
Noah found that grace.

No one escapes Divine judgment except by grace.
It does not say he found grace in the eyes of men, but in
the eyes of God. Even though there were **"men of
renown,"** God had a servant in the land, a true giant of
the faith.

Noah was righteous, blameless, and he walked
with God. Righteous means He was accepted based on
sacrifice and covenant. This is the first time in Scripture
where God calls someone **"righteous."** We are made
righteous by faith (Rom. 5:1). This is why Noah is included in the list of fifteen believers mentioned in the great
faith chapter (Heb. 11).

"Blameless" is in reference to how we are in our
dealings with our fellowman. Blameless is the Hebrew
term used in Leviticus for 'without blemish' or 'not con-
taminated.' Most importantly, Noah walked in fellow-

ship with God. It is only as we walk with God that we are kept from the evil of our age.

Hebrews 11:7 tells us much about Noah: *"By faith Noah, when warned about things not yet seen, in holy fear built an ark to save his family. By faith he condemned the world and became heir of the righteousness that comes by faith."* Note the faith of Noah:

- The **BASIS** of his faith—God's Word . . . *warned"* by God.

- The **EXTENT** of his faith—laid hold of *"things not yet seen."*

- The **VIRTUE** of his faith—built the ark *"in holy fear."*

- The **EVIDENCE** of his faith—*"built an ark to save his family."*

- The **WITNESS** of his faith—*"By faith he condemned the world."*

- The **REWARD** of his faith—Noah *"became heir of the righteousness that comes by faith."*

In contrast to Noah, the earth was corrupt and filled with violence. These verses give us a graphic picture of human nature at its worst (Ps. 14:1-5). **"God saw how corrupt the earth had become, for all the people on earth had corrupted their ways."** Senseless violence, corruption and wickedness, demonic offspring roaming the earth—the Lord God was moved to destroy the earth.

God spoke to Noah and warned him of the Flood and the means of escape. How did God speak to him? Did He come in human form? Perhaps He appeared in a burning bush, or as an angel, or in a dream? God is able to speak in whatever way He chooses. We have a God who speaks to those whose ways are blameless. Noah moved with faith and acted on the revelation given to him. Do you respond when God speaks?

In verses 14-22 we are given the details for the building of the Ark and Noah's obedience to God's commands. Noah's Ark clearly speaks of the Lord Jesus Christ. Just as Noah's ARK delivered his family from the Flood, so Jesus delivers those who believe in Him from the wrath of God. My Jesus is an ARK!

The materials and dimensions of the Ark are given below:

◆ The Ark was made of cypress wood, which speaks of the HUMANITY of our Lord Jesus.

◆ The Ark was 450 ft. long, 75 ft. wide and 45 ft. tall.[1]

◆ The Ark had only one door—only ONE SAVIOR (John 10:9, 14:6).

◆ The door was set in the SIDE of the Ark—Jesus was PIERCED in His SIDE (John 19:34).

◆ The Ark had three levels—Jesus provides salvation for body, soul, and spirit (1 Thess. 5:23).

◆ There was a window giving light in the third loft—we look up to Jesus (Col. 3:3).

◆ There were many rooms (nests)—*"In my Father's house are many rooms"* (John 14:2).

◆ The Ark was coated inside and out with pitch (Heb. 'atonement') as a symbol of the blood of Christ that atones for sin and delivers us from judgment.[2]

◆ The Ark endured the fury of the Flood—Christ endured the wrath of God for us (Ps. 42:7).

◆ The Ark was God's provision for Noah—Christ is God's provision for sinners.

"I am going to put an end to all people." We must always remember that God was long-suffering with man before He determined to destroy the earth. God waited a long time in mercy before the Ark was shut. How long did He wait? Nine hundred sixty-nine years! The birth of Methuselah was a prophecy of coming judgment.

Methuselah's name means, 'when he dies it (judgment) will come.' The longest living human was Methuselah. For almost one thousand years God was long-suffering with man waiting for him to repent and walk with God. Mercy postponed judgment. *"God waited patiently in the days of Noah while the ark was being built"* (1 Pet. 3:20).

Lest we feel that God was mistaken when He judged the earth, note the revelation that was given to the people of the world before judgment day came:

1. They had the light of the created world (Rom. 1:19,20).

2. They were given the Promise of a Redeemer (Gen. 3:15).

3. They had been taught of blood sacrifice through the "coats of skins" and Abel's offering.

4. There was the continual reminder of judgment by the "mark of Cain" seen on his forehead.

5. The prophecy of Enoch, the birth of Methuselah, and the strange disappearance of Enoch.

6. The preaching of Noah and the building of the Ark (2 Pet. 2:25).

7. The ministry of the Holy Spirit striving with hearts (Gen. 6:3).

Divine revelation had been despised and rejected. They did not know what was coming. In spite of what God was speaking, they deliberately persisted in wickedness. They were without excuse. With their sins stacked up to the heavens, God determined to wipe out the inhabitants of the earth by a worldwide flood. This judgment would cleanse the earth of its wickedness and give Noah a fresh start. To Noah God said, **"I will establish my covenant with you."** (6:18)

God gives a solemn promise to Noah, guaranteeing his preservation and security. Noah was convinced by this covenant that God would keep His Word. God gives him instructions regarding the animals coming two by two into the ark; and regarding the necessary food to preserve them. God told Noah ahead of time what was going to happen. We have no record that from that time until Genesis 7:1 God ever spoke to him again. That could have been up to 120 years.

Consider Noah: Knowing the end of the age was upon him he faithfully preached for 120 years without affirmation, applause, or approval from anyone on earth. He saw as a prophet the dreadful wrath of God coming to the earth; his ears heard the terrifying cries of an entire civilization coming to their doom. What burdens did he carry? How did he process the catastrophic destruction of all those outside the ark?

God lists Noah in Ezekiel 14:14 with Daniel and Job . . . men who stood fast against all opposition in the face of the king and other leaders, in the face of roaring lions and roaring disappointments. Daniel and Job were overcomers. They each stood fast in the face of so much physical oppression, the loss of their family and their wealth, along with great emotional pressure.

Noah moved with holy fear in building the ark (Heb. 11:7). This was one of the most heroic acts of faith recorded in Scripture as he endured the scorn and pity of the ungodly. By calculating the dates of these events, scholars conclude that Noah's sons were born twenty years after he was given these instructions. The flood came 1,656 years after Adam was made by God's hand. . . .

"Go into the ark"

Noah's ark was not a prison, but a refuge and a hiding place from the storm of judgment—so is the Lord Jesus Christ. Christ is our Ark of Refuge. He is ready to receive all that come to Him. God saw Noah as **"righteous in this generation."** The Lord knows those that are

His. Those who keep themselves pure in times of wickedness, God will keep safe in times of judgment.

All the animals had been placed under the dominion of man at creation (Gen. 1:26). To Noah was given the charge of taking the animals, male and female, into the preserving confines of the ark. He led into the ark seven pairs of every kind of **"clean"** animal and two of every kind of **"unclean"** animal . . . All of this was to be done within seven days. The clean animals were to be for sacrifices and for food after leaving the ark. Some calculate that there was room for over seven thousand species of animals.

For 120 years Noah preached righteousness to his generation. The descendants of Cain built a city. Noah built an ark. Now the time had come for the animals to be supernaturally drawn to the ark. God's drawing power brought the multitude of these animals to the door of the ark in only seven days! This was quite a miracle. Only God could subdue the beasts of the earth and cause them to enter the confines of this floating zoo. This would have been an amazing sight to the unbelievers of his day who witnessed the hundreds of animals streaming into Noah's neighborhood. This was the visible conclusion to the sermon Noah had preached for 120 years. We wonder why they didn't join Noah inside this ark of safety!

During these seven days there was no sight of rain, or storm—no reason to suspect that judgment was imminent. Yet Noah moved with holy fear and prepared them all to ride out the storm. He moved by faith when the warning of God was spoken. **"In the six hundredth year of Noah's life, on the seventeenth day of the second month—on that day all the springs of the great deep** burst forth, and the floodgates of the heavens were opened. And rain fell on the earth forty days and forty nights."

The aged Noah had served God faithfully. As the waters burst forth to cleanse the earth of its wickedness, Noah and his sons and their wives were spared. By calculating the months, this would have been either October or November. God waited until after the produce of the earth could be gathered in to feed the animals and their caretakers.

"All the springs of the great deep burst forth." From beneath the surface giant fissures broke open with massive amounts of subterranean waters bursting forth.[3] *"He puts the deep into storehouses"* (Ps. 33:7). These *"storehouses"* or reservoirs sprang up and flooded the earth.

God, at creation, had fixed a *"boundary,"* setting *"doors and bars in place"* that the waters could not pass (Job 38:8-11, Ps. 104:9). Now He simply removes those restraints and the waters gush forth to flood the earth as they had done at first (Gen. 1:9). The **"floodgates of the heavens"** were similarly opened up.

This was a true cloudburst (Job 26:8, 37:11)! For forty days and forty nights, without stopping, the awesome judgments of God were poured out upon all the earth. He made the earth in six days; He takes forty to destroy it! It is impossible to escape the righteous judgments of God when we resist His warnings (Job 20:27). Who is able to stand before God when He is angry?

In this destruction of the world by water, God gives us a solemn warning that He will again judge the wickedness of man. Not by water, but by fire (2 Pet. 3:4-7). As there are waters under the earth, we know also there is FIRE under the earth that can spew forth at any time. From beneath and from the heavens, fire will be released to purge the earth of all its sin. Are you ready? What will keep you safe from judgment fires?

---

[1] These dimensions equal 33,750 square feet per floor times three floors. If you measure it by the cubic foot, it is 1,400,000 cubic feet, more than 450 feet long, displacing 18,000 tons (about one and a half football fields)! In proportion, this would be the dimension of a Man...

[2] "Pitch" is a gummy, sticky substance that waterproofs the ark. Interestingly, this is not the word usually used for pitch. It is used seventy other times in the Old Testament as "atonement."

[3] In this pre-flood time there was a canopy surrounding the entire earth. As most creationist geologists believe, if there were oceans at that time they were very shallow. Underneath the earth's crust were subterranean waters which fed the four rivers around the Garden of Eden. The canopy overhead provided a barrier from cosmic ray bombardment. Yet, evidently the subterranean waters heated up until they simply burst up through the earth's crust. At the same time the canopy of water collapsed. As the crust burst with water and magma and lava, and ash filled the air, it was a tremendous cataclysm.

CHAPTER ELEVEN

THE RAIN & THE RAINBOW

"Then the LORD shut him in"

Elohim "commanded" and Jehovah shut Noah in to protect and preserve. Notice the two names of God: Elohim ('the Mighty One') and Jehovah (the Covenant Keeping God, the Friend of sinners). God is the common Name and Jehovah is the name of intimacy and friendship. It was the Lord Jehovah who shut the door (Gen. 7:16), to secure Noah from the waters of judgment, and to keep out those who believed too late. For at least seven days the door of the ark stood open. All could come if they would forsake their sin and believe.

When God shut the door none could open it. Very soon, the door of mercy will again be shut for all humanity. Now is the time to warn others, for the time will come when they will knock and the door will NOT be opened to them!

What terror seized their hearts as they realized that old Noah was right and that they were wrong. Surrounded by judgment with no place to hide—what horrors await those who reject the mercy of God! Those who will drown in their lusts and sensuality and vice will also drown in the judgment of Almighty God (Prov. 1:24,25).

"The waters rose and covered the mountains to a depth of more than twenty feet." Water covered the earth to a depth of over three miles! The mountains departed and the hills were removed but God's covenant of peace with Noah remained (Isa. 54:10). Who was it that measured the waters out in His hand? Who was it that knew the mountains were covered more than twenty feet? Noah could not—he couldn't get out of the ark to measure it! It was God.

Never did death triumph like it did on this day. The flood came and took them all away (Matt. 24:19). **"Every living thing that moved on the earth perished."** The universal flood destroyed all of the unbelieving. God is just in all His works. He, who made man as He pleases, may destroy man as He pleases. Who are we to question the mighty works of God? God did what was right. The earth was corrupt. The plan of God was being thwarted. There must be a new beginning. We too, will be swept away by our sins if we do not repent and believe the gospel.

Pause and ponder this tremendous judgment. Can we now see and say, "It is a dreadful thing to fall into the hands of the living God" (Heb. 10:31). It is an evil thing, and bitter, to depart from God. Who can stand before His anger? Who can quench judgment fires when His holiness is provoked?

"Only Noah was left and those with him in the ark" (Gen. 7:23). Thousands fell on his right hand, ten thousand at his left, but Noah lives. Mercy triumphed over judgment. The saving grace of God prevailed for his household. *"Surely when the mighty waters rise, they will not reach him"* (Ps. 32:6). Only Noah was left. Even the godly

Noah delivered only himself and his family (Ezek. 14:14). Righteousness delivers from death (Prov. 10:2, 11:6). Truly, Noah found favor in the eyes of the Lord.

"But God remembered Noah"

How faithful and merciful is God to Noah! Mercy is returning to the earth. To say that God remembered Noah is not to imply that Noah was ever forgotten. God's heart was turned again to the one who found favor with Him (Luke 1:72). God is about to fulfill all His promises to Noah. The fury of God's wrath against sinful man subsides. Mercy rises in the heart of Elohim. Noah is not forgotten (Isa. 49:15,16). In wrath, God remembered mercy (Hab. 3:2).

God commanded the wind to blow, causing the waters to recede (Ps. 148:8). Perhaps this was the same wind that God sent to part the waters of the Red Sea (Ex. 14:21). He sealed up the springs of the deep and closed the floodgates of heaven—God alone holds those keys. For 150 days the waters had flooded the earth, now it was time to dry it up. The world had been baptized in judgment, now the beams of the sun kissed the earth again.

We are so quick to view this story as merely a story of judgment but it contains a greater theme; the saving grace of God. Certainly, death and destruction prevailed at the time of the Flood, but so does mercy. In every act of judgment there is mercy if we look for it.

The ark rested on the **"seventeenth day of the seventh month."** The commandment of the Lord given at the institution of the Feast of Passover changed the seventh month to the first month for Israel. Passover was the fourteenth day of the month. Three days later would be the seventeenth day of the month; the very day Jesus rose from the dead. The final resting place of our ARK of salvation was the top of the mountain. Jesus was raised on high, seated at the right hand of the Most High. What inspiration lies within the Bible!

Noah sent forth a raven through the window of the ark while the waters receded. The unclean bird likely fed on the floating carcasses of men and beasts. Then he sent forth a dove that promptly returned, signifying that dry land had not yet appeared. After seven days the dove was again released, returning with an olive leaf in its beak, proving to Noah that the trees had begun to appear. After another seven days the dove was released and did not return—finding rest upon dry land.

The raven and the dove speak of the two natures of the believer. The raven is unclean, a type of the fallen, corrupt nature of every person. The raven fed on death and decay . . . to be fleshly minded is death (Rom. 8:6). The carnal mind can rest on anything and everything but Christ.

The three outgoings of the dove from the ark are a symbolic picture of the work of the Holy Spirit in human history. The *first* time the dove was sent out, it fluttered over the dirty waters, but having no place to rest, it returned to the ark. So in the ages before Jesus the Holy Spirit went forth throughout all of humanity but did not find a resting place. He touched men here and there, but He did not abide upon them. Abraham, David, Isaiah all knew the touch of the Spirit but not the abiding presence . . . He could not build a nest in the hearts of men so He returned to the heart of the Father.

The *second* time the dove went forth it did find something. The Holy Spirit came upon Jesus at His baptism and planted the BRANCH on the earth. The olive branch grew into a cross, where peace and pardon flow to fallen ones . . . On the cross, the floodwaters of judgment abate and dry up. . . .

The dove returning with the olive branch speaks of the Spirit of God bringing life and peace to the soul (Jesus is the Branch Man, Jer. 33, Zech. 6, and John 15). The Dove (Holy Spirit) cannot rest where there is corruption and death. For generations the Dove sought a place to rest. It flew over Abraham, Moses, the Prophets—until at last at the River Jordan, the Dove came from the open heaven and rested on the Perfect Man, JESUS the Son of God (Matt. 3:16).

A third time the dove flew from the ark . . . On the day of Pentecost the world was ready for the abiding presence of the dove! The floods are gone . . . there is a place now ready in the hearts of men for a nest. He has now come, not as a fluttering guest, but as the abiding presence. He has come to build a nest and rear His young. Has the gentle dove found a nest (Gal. 5:22,23) in your heart?

God's Covenant with Noah (8:15-22)

Noah spent approximately one year in the ark. Five months floating and seven months on the mountain! God give us the patience of Noah! Noah did not stir until God spoke to him. This man was obedient to God, refusing to move until he heard the Word of the Lord. Just as he waited for the command to enter, he waits for the command to disembark.

You know that it had to be hard to float around with thousands of smelly animals for a year. Faith will wait until God speaks. Finding grace in God's eyes does not free us to do as we please. We are under His government.

Noah and his family would never forget the moment they pushed open the door of the ark and walked out into a new world. Eight human beings found a new beginning with God. Like a new Adam and a new Eve they began all over again. What a spine-tingling moment it was! The bright sunlight, the fresh air, the gentle breeze . . . God had seen them through!

"Then Noah built an altar unto the Lord." In humble gratitude, he worships at the altar as he offers sacrifice to God. Brought out into a cold and desolate world, Noah did not build a house; he built an altar . . . the first altar in Scripture. Noah worships where there was only a scene of death and desolation. The true worshipper knows they have escaped catastrophe. God accepts our worship when mercy pierces our heart.

This sacrifice was an act of praise and submission to God. The smoke of the sacrifice curled up into the approving blue sky. God was pleased. Noah realized God's fixed purpose is to bring man from sin into righteousness based on sacrifice. Noah confessed the evil that was in him and, like Abel, brought a pleasing sacrifice to God. Elohim starts over with this spared family . . . a worshipping community.

He offered burnt offerings from the stock of clean animals that came off the ark. Noah did not tithe; he gave a seventh to God. God viewed this sacrifice as a **"pleasing aroma."** The Hebrew word is 'an aroma of rest.' This sacrifice caused the Father to rest. What was it about the sacrifice of the seventh that pleased God? Jesus Christ is the SEVENTH MAN whose sacrifice was an aroma of rest to God's heart. It satisfied and stirred the Father. God declares that He will never again completely destroy man and animal.

So painful was the flood to God and so beautiful was the sacrifice of Noah, that it moved the Father's heart to speak these words. God has pity toward mankind, even though every inclination of his heart is evil from childhood (Ps. 78:38,39, 103:8-14). The mercy of God is revealed by this covenant with mankind. As long as the earth endures, God will faithfully provide for man all his days. GRACE is greater than our sin. MERCY has triumphed over judgment.

This covenant promise of God was based on sacrifice (8:20,22, Eph. 5:2). The annual fulfillment of this covenant through the centuries forms a striking demonstration of God's faithfulness. A covenant is an oath of promise made between God and man. There are seven covenants made by God in Scripture:

1. God's Covenant with **ADAM** (Gen. 3).
2. God's Covenant with **NOAH** (Gen. 8-9).
3. God's Covenant with **ABRAHAM** (Gen. 15).
4. God's Covenant with **MOSES** and Israel (Ex. 20-34).
5. God's Covenant with **LEVI** and the priesthood (Num. 25, Ezek. 44:15, Mal. 2:4,5).
6. God's Covenant with **DAVID** (2 Sam. 23, 2 Chron. 13).
7. God's **NEW COVENANT** with His Church—ratified by His blood (Matt. 26:28).

After living in the Ark for a year, Noah's life involved an altar and a tent. He did not build a city but an altar . . . and lived in a tent. Noah's tent with the altar outside was a preview of the coming Tabernacle with the altar for the burnt offering. God lived with Noah in his tent. . . .

"Then God blessed Noah and his sons."

God blesses Noah and his sons as the new heads of humanity. The human race begins again with the blessing and goodwill of God upon their lives. A new era of human existence begins with this charter or covenant given to Noah:

♦ They are commanded to multiply and fill the earth.

♦ Power will be given over the animals.

♦ They are given permission to eat the flesh of living creatures. Every creature of God is now good for food (1 Tim. 4:4). Evidently, prior to the flood man was a vegetarian.

We are reminded every time we eat meat that we are living because of the death of another. Every time you eat meat, you are eating it because an animal gave its life. It is almost as if God gives us meat to eat to remind us that physically we live by the death of another, and *spiritually* we live by the death of another. We live spiritually because God's Son gave His life for us. He shed His blood. We eat meat because some animal shed his blood for us.

Two warnings are given: **1)** They are told not to eat raw flesh with blood; **2)** Man must not take away the life of another. Capital punishment is instituted for any man or beast that kills a human being. Willful murderers must be put to death (2 Chron. 24:22). God now commits the administration of justice to humankind. God teaches man about justice by giving him the authority to take life. When Cain killed Abel, Cain was not slain. God did not kill Cain but gave him a life sentence. When Lamech slew a man, no one killed Lamech. But now, man will act on behalf of God in showing His justice (Rom. 13:1-4).

God places supreme value upon human life, made in His image. To deface the King's image is a form of treason among men. Murder is much more than an act of hostility against man; it is an affront against the One who made us in His image. God teaches us to safeguard human life. Since the life of man is in the blood, and a fetus has blood, a fetus has life . . . it is murder to kill an unborn baby.

CHAPTER TWELVE

THE RAINBOW COVENANT

"I will see the bow . . ."

There were no negotiations between God and Noah; God alone dictated the terms. The Lord's covenant is that a worldwide flood will never again destroy the earth (Isa. 54:9). In Chapter 9, God uses the word 'covenant' seven times. That is a divine number. He uses it in verses 9, 11, 12, 13, 15, 16, 17. In all, counting 6:18, God mentions His rainbow covenant to Noah eight times. Seven is the number of fullness; eight, the number of a new beginning.

Perhaps you can imagine the fear they would have had at the first sign of a thunderstorm! The SEAL of this covenant was the rainbow in the clouds. This **"bow"** is without arrows. The unstrung bow in the sky is a sign of peace and freedom that God hangs over the human race. The bow in the clouds was not only a promise that God would not destroy the earth with a flood, but it was a token of a new relationship.

"I will see it," God declared as He put a rainbow in the clouds for you! God is light. The rainbow is the light and glory of God revealed in faithfulness to mankind. The rainbow is the reflection of the beams of the sun, showing the excellency of this covenant comes from the glory of the "sun of righteousness," (Mal. 4:2, Ezek. 1:28, Rev. 4:3,11).

The seven colors of the rainbow represent the fullness of the Spirit appearing in the earth. The revelation of the Spirit is seen in seven colors or a seven-fold manifestation (Rev. 4:5).

Purple—*Royalty*, Jesus is the King (1 Tim. 6:15).

Blue—*Heaven*, Jesus came down from heaven (John 3:13).

Green—*New life*, Jesus gives life to us all (John 14:6).

Yellow—*Brightness of the sun*, Jesus is the Light (John 8:12).

Orange—*The amber glow of glory*, Jesus is the Glory!

Red—*Blood*, the blood of Jesus washes away sin (Rev. 1:5).

As the rainbow is the union of heaven and earth—spanning the sky and reaching the earth, so is Jesus; who brings together man and God. As the rainbow is a public sign in the heavens, so the *"grace of God that brings salvation has appeared to all men"* through His Son (Titus 2:11). All peoples everywhere see the rainbow; the covenant-sign. All people must have the chance to believe in Christ.

God hung up His battle bow to be a sign of peace. God's covenant has turned judgment into grace. He remembers His Covenant, not our sin! This is the sweet message of *"no condemnation for those who are in Christ Jesus"* (Rom. 8:1).

We have a covenant better than a rainbow—the precious promises of Christ! His grace can take the storm clouds and teardrops of our lives and turn them into arches of triumph and glorious jewels. The half-arch of the rainbow will one day become a full circle going around the throne (Rev. 4:3). Only those in the glory can see the full rainbow of His throne!

The blood given to ratify the New Covenant overshadows all the covenants of the Old Testament. However, the prophets of the Old Testament did refer to the Noahic Covenant. Notice how they use similar language as that found in Genesis 9:

> *For this is like the days of Noah to Me; when I swore that the waters of Noah should not flood the earth again, so I have sworn that I will not be angry with you, nor will I rebuke you. For the mountains may be removed and the hills may shake, but My loving-kindness will not be removed from you, and My covenant of peace will not be shaken, says the Lord who has compassion on you.*
>
> **Isaiah 54:9,10**

> *"In that day I will also make a covenant for them withthe beasts of the field, the birds of the sky, and the creeping things of the ground . . ."* **(Hosea 2:18).**

The Sin of Noah (9:20-29)

Noah had been a carpenter while building the ark, now he becomes a farmer. In the first garden, Adam fell. In the second garden, Noah fell. Noah harvested grapes and called a celebration of feasting with his family. His sin was not just that He got drunk and forgot to put his clothes on.

The Hebrew text infers that it was a deliberate act of nudity. Some scholars conclude that Ham's sin was homosexual activity with his father. Interestingly, Moses, the author of Genesis, seems to keep the details of this sin private . . . perhaps we should learn a lesson from that also. We are all a fallen people, regardless of how many blessings we have. Man is unable to stand without grace. Notice the similarity between Adam and Noah:

♦ They both came forth after the earth emerged from water (1:12).

♦ They both were made lords over creation (1:28).

♦ They both were blessed and told to multiply (1:28).

♦ They both worked in a garden.

♦ They both were tempted and fell in a garden/vineyard.

♦ Their sin resulted in nakedness (3:7).

♦ Both had their nakedness covered by another.

♦ Their sin brought a great curse to their descendants.

♦ After their fall, they both were given a prophecy of redemption.

♦ Both had three sons, one of whom would produce the Messiah.

Ham sins by not covering his naked father. To expose and sneer at his father's fall was wickedness of the worst kind. Ham failed to honor his father, lacking covering love (1 Pet. 4:8). Had he really cared for his father he would have covered him with the robe of reverence, as did Shem and Japheth.

The sin nature of humanity loves to see those in authority exposed to shame, for it gives them a false freedom from restriction and gives them an excuse for their sin. . . .

(our character)

The failure of Noah becomes a test for his sons. Many times the failures of our leaders are a test of our response. Apart from Jesus Christ, there are no perfect leaders, only imperfect. Your boss, your pastor, your best friend, your mother and father . . . all are imperfect. When we expose those over us to dishonor and humiliation, it brings a curse. Proverbs 30:17 states, *"The eye that mocks a father, that scorns obedience to a mother, will be pecked out by the ravens of the valley, will be eaten by the vultures."*

Clothing in the Scripture is a type of righteousness (Rev. 19:8). Ham, by the course he followed, showed he knew nothing of the covering of righteousness that is ours by faith. Shem and Japheth exhibited, in their actions, the Divine method of dealing with human nakedness. Because they covered their father, they inherit a blessing.

Noah then prophesies over his three sons, giving an outline sketch of the history of the nations. The great races of people are seen in their embryonic condition. There is far more in Noah's words than an expression of indignation. Noah's words are a prophecy over his sons and the nations they represent.

When Noah awoke from his stupor he discovered what Ham had done. Instead of cursing his son, he cursed Canaan, Ham's son. Why didn't Noah curse Ham instead of Ham's son? Noah knew that Canaan would dishonor Ham just as Noah had been dishonored by Ham . . . that would be his curse! The sins of the father would be passed on to his son.

The descendants of Ham became slaves. How you relate to the shortcomings of your superiors touches your children and your children's children. Those who dishonor and reject authority will eventually become slaves. Canaan would now become the servant of Shem (9:26) and Japheth (9:27).

The curse was that the descendants of Canaan (the 'Canaanites') would be subject to the Hebrew descendants of Shem (Josh. 9:23, Judges 1). They were eventually to be driven out of the land given to the Jews. God could have appointed Ham for leadership, instead, because of his sin, he becomes a servant.

The curse on Canaan eventually affected an entire territory. His descendants would one day populate an area along the Mediterranean coast and establish two cities named Sodom and Gomorrah. The rampant homosexuality (the generational curse brought on by Ham) would prompt God to destroy them. Entire regions may be affected by generational curses. A territorial iniquity can take root and make those who dwell there susceptible to its power.

Shem's prophecy was that Jehovah would now be the God of Shem in a unique way, mingling His name with Shem's (Shem = "name"). This is a prophecy that a descendant of Shem would be Jehovah incarnate. Jesus Christ descended from Shem! Shem's reward was that he would be the ancestor of Christ. The God of Shem is blessed as the Covenant Keeper. The descendants of Japheth may have enlargement, but Shem has God.

Japheth would be blessed with widespread increase and influence. Japheth means 'enlargement.' This one word of prophetic blessing has carried over even to this day. Japheth dwelling in the tents of Shem speaks of the blessing of Shem that would be shared with Japheth.[1] There would be peaceful coexistence between them. Japheth would enlarge his habitation throughout the earth.

This prophecy from Noah, the builder of the Ark, gives in a few words a brief history of the world. The three great divisions of the human family, descending from Noah's sons are mentioned in this prophecy. Interestingly, all three sons of Noah were generationally present at the crucifixion of the Lord Jesus. The descendants of Shem were present in the Jewish religious leaders who wanted the Messiah dead and out of the way. Japheth was present in the Romans who participated jointly with the Jews to crucify the Lord Jesus. And a descendant of Ham was present in the person of Simon of Cyrene, who bore the cross of Christ in servitude (Luke 23:26).

The sons of Noah are brought before us again in Acts 8-10. The Ethiopian eunuch was a descendant of Ham and was blessed with the gospel (Acts 8). Saul of Tarsus (Paul) was from Shem, also converted by the revelation of Jesus (Acts 9). Cornelius the centurion was a son of Japheth who believed the good news of Christ (Acts 10).

The Table of Nations (Genesis 10)

This chapter presents us with the earliest ethnological table in the literature of the ancient world. This remarkable Table of Nations gives us a perception of the ethnic and linguistic situation of the age of Noah and his descendants.

It must be stated clearly: God is King of the nations (Ps. 82:8, 96:7-10, Jer. 10:7). He rules over the earth and judges the nations when they forget Him (Ps. 7:8). The ancient teachers in Israel taught the Hebrews that God assigned an angel to be the angel of every nation. These messengers from God hold the vision of what that nation is meant to become . . . until all the nations worship the Lord, their Creator.

Virtually ALL of these names have been found in the archeological discoveries of the past one hundred years. This chapter is so incredibly accurate, nothing can compare to its historical integrity. Genesis 10 is a structured arrangement of the most important nations of the ancient world.

From Noah and his three sons descended all the nations and peoples of the world. The human race really is one family. We all have the same father, Noah. Divided by language, territory, and politics we are placed together on this planet to learn the ways of God and love one another.

Japheth is followed by seven sons (nations), understood by many to be the Caucasian peoples. The total of names listed here comes to seventy, the same number of Israelites that came into Egypt at the time of Joseph.

Jesus sent out seventy disciples to preach the kingdom of God. Perhaps this could be considered God's first statement that He is concerned about foreign missions! Note the nations divided by family listed below:

Gomer (v.2) the father of the Gauls or Gallic peoples, (i.e. CELTS).

Magog (v.2) the peoples of the Ukraine, Scythians.

Madai (v.2) the Medes, Persians and related groups, Elamites.

Javan (v.2) the Hebrew name for Greeks or Tartars.

Meshech (v.2) or Moscow.[2]

Tiran (v.2) or Tirana—the people who settled in the Balkans, Romania, Bulgaria, & Moravia.

Ashkenaz (v.3) settled near the Black Sea and was the father of the Scandinavians and the Saxon and Germanic peoples.

Togarmah (v.3) is most likely modern TURKEY. Also includes Azerbaijan, Uzbekistan & Kazakhstan.

Tarshish (v.4) is a possible reference to Tartessus, ancient SPAIN.

Maritime peoples (v.5) who lived on the islands of the sea.

Cush (v.6) is Ethiopia.

Mizraim (v.6) is today's Egypt, called the land of Ham in Psalms 78:51, 105:23, 27.

Put (v.6) or "Phut" corresponds to modern day Libya.

Dedan (v.7) is considered by many to be modern Kuwait.

Aram (v.22) is Syria. Jesus spoke the Aramaic language.

Eber (v.24) was father of the Hebrews, Abraham's ancestor.

Peleg (v.25) means 'division' but in Greek means 'sea.' (Note the English word 'archi-*pelago*')[3]

---

[1] Some scholars see in this prophecy a coming day when the blessings of Shem would come to the Gentiles (the "one new man", the church).

[2] Many think RUSSIA is modern Magog, Tubal, and Meshech referred to in Ezekiel 38:2.

[3] The Greeks call the Agean Sea 'the Archipelago,' the first sea. There is some evidence to link this with the scientific theory of continental drift; the parting of the continents during the days of Peleg.

CHAPTER THIRTEEN

NIMROD

"Nimrod, a mighty hunter before the Lord"

The man NIMROD[1] is introduced as an Ethiopian, whose name means, 'rebel.' He grew to be a mighty warrior on the earth, the first of the heroic conquerors. Nimrod was ambitious, aspiring to be over others. This self-promoting spirit controlled him. Walking in pride and tyranny he soon became a **"mighty hunter"** before the Lord. This implies he was a violent invader of other's rights and properties.

Nimrod was a terrorist! The Septuagint text reads, 'he was a mighty hunter *against* the Lord.' As a terrorist, Nimrod became a mighty ruler over others, laying the foundations of a monarchy. He had no God-given right or command to rule, he simply took it upon himself to govern by fear and force.

The word used here for **"mighty"** means 'chief' or 'chieftain.' He was the most outstanding leader in the four hundred years between the flood and Abraham. Nimrod was also a man who developed false worship (Babel). Babylonia was long known as the 'Land of Nimrod.'

Nimrod built a kingdom . . . the kingdom of this world. Cities were constructed under his rule. His one aim was to make for himself a name. He is a type of the Man of Sin, the Antichrist prophesied to come (2 Thess. 2:4-9). His ambition was to make a worldwide kingdom for himself. How destructive is this spirit when released among men! It can destroy a church, even nations.

The Canaanite clans were scattered throughout the land that God would soon give to Abram and his descendants (v. 15-19). The borders listed trace out the Promised Land.

Eber is the fourth generation after Shem and the ancestor of all the Hebrew peoples . . . from which the SPIRITUAL SEED would one day arise. . . .

"Now the whole world had one language."

Genesis 1-9 covered a time span of centuries and millenniums. It included creation, worldwide judgment, and God's worldwide program. Chapters 10 and 11 begin to focus on one specific family. In this chapter we will be introduced to a descendant of Eber, a man named Abram. . . .

As the descendants of Noah multiplied, the earth was filled with a people of one language. This common language could have been used to worship the Creator and sing His praises. But sadly, God's gift of language was misused.

As men moved westward (turning their backs on the sunrise), they found a plain in Shinar or **"Babylon."** Dwelling together as one in what is today Iraq they built a tower of bricks. This brick tower was for the worship of pagan deities. Uniting as one glorious empire, with ambitious Nimrod as the Head, mankind was again defiant of God.

Not content to build numerous cities, Nimrod sought to build one that would tower above them all. This pagan metropolis was a vain attempt to deify man and his accomplishments. They did not want to be scattered in defiance to God's command to "replenish the earth" (Gen. 9:1). The sons of Noah traded their tent for a townhouse. . . .

Just as Lucifer sought to exalt himself above the heavens, so fallen man seeks to build this tower into the heavens. Babel-builders today seek the same thing. Man is ambitious, seeking greatness. We erect our cities, our systems of commerce, even religious institutions; yet at heart of much of these 'towers' is selfish ambition; the desire to make OUR names great; making a name to deny God's Name.

An ancient historian, Philo Judaeus, says that each one engraved their names upon the bricks to memorialize themselves. Today their names are forgotten and the Name of God stands as a High Tower.

Seeking to make a name for ourselves is self-worship. We are to lay aside our reputation to make the Name of Jesus famous (Phil. 2:3-11). Jesus made Himself of no reputation. Why would we seek to make our name great (Jer. 45:5)? Every Babel we erect will be turned to confusion (Babel means 'confusion').

There is no mention of seeking God, or waiting upon Him for direction. Out of the ambitious schemes of man, this tower of confusion was erected. Babylon is a picture of this world system that has no room for the Living God. But the Lord came down to see the city and the tower they built for themselves.

God comes to them in human form. So Jesus Christ, the Son of God, came down to this earth to see the works of our lives and carry our judgment to His Cross (Ps. 113:5,6). God comes to frustrate this worldwide conspiracy to unite the nations of the earth under one government. He comes to *"look at every proud man and bring them low"* (Job 40:11-14).

On top of the tower, and on its ceiling and walls, were star charts and the signs of the zodiac. Scholars and encyclopedias admit that astrology began in Babylon. Behind the four-footed beasts, behind the birds, behind the men, lurked the real host of the heavens whose leader is the daystar, Lucifer. The purpose of the tower was to worship the stars, the host of heaven. Eventually an elite group of priests and priestesses developed. This select group were the only ones with the knowledge of how to worship the stars. Sexual mythology began to enter in. The priestesses became prostitutes and the priests became male prostitutes. By the time of Joshua it ended with full-blown Baalism in the land of Canaan.

The people made bricks. God's building never includes bricks, only *stones*. Man makes bricks; God is the Maker of stones. The New Jerusalem will not be made from bricks but from precious *stones* (Rev. 21:18-20). Pharaoh made his treasure cities out of bricks.

Out of their rebellion, they decided to use what their hands could make to erect a city made with hands. Soon, the Eternal City will be seen that is NOT made by hands!

The church is built together with the Living Stones of those who love the Lord Jesus.

God's judgment of Babel resulted in the confusion of their language. They speak thousands of different languages as confusion reigns. A man would think one thing and say another because God had changed the brain centers and the vocal chords.

At first, perhaps, each thought the other was mocking him. Soon fighting would begin, reaching the point where those who spoke the same language got together and said, "Let's leave. We can't live here." So the scattering began. Evidently one small group stayed behind near Ur of the Chaldees. That is the group whose genealogy continues.

The multitude of languages today is a monument to sin. Unity in the Spirit of God brings a common speech . . . Jesus is the Word, the language of God! Pentecost reversed this judgment. The nations of the earth heard each man speaking in their own language as they were enabled by the Holy Spirit (Acts 2). One day all languages will gather around the LAMB in glorified praise to Him. Perhaps the religious confusion of multiple denominations is a sign that man is still seeking to build kingdoms without the wisdom and unity of the Holy Spirit.

The Generations from the Flood to Abram (11:10-32)

Notice the decreasing life span of those listed here. Shem lived 600 years, Arphaxad 438, Salah 433, Peleg 239 years, Serug 230, Nahor 148. Perhaps this is because the vapor canopy that once covered the earth before the flood is now removed.

From Shem to Abraham we cover ten generations (427 years from the Flood to Abraham). Noah died two years before Abraham was born. Note the mention of EBER (11:14) which is the root word for HEBREW. At last we come to Terah and his three sons—Abram, Nahor, and Haran, the father of Lot (and grandfather of Rebekah).

The family home of Terah was Ur of the Chaldeans,[2] a major city located north of the Persian Gulf. At 2,000 B.C. it was the greatest city in the world. While the family clan was still in Ur, Haran died, leaving Lot fatherless. While still in Ur, Abram married Sarai (Sarah) and she remained barren for many years to come.

(Terah-an idol maker)· Converts (through Abram)

Terah and other members of Abram's clan were idol worshippers (Josh. 24:2). Ur was named after the moon goddess and was the center of worship. The Chaldeans were astrologers, occultists, and idol worshippers. Ancient traditions state that Terah was an idol-maker until his death. The Jewish writers have a tradition that Abram was cast into a fiery furnace for refusing to worship idols, and was miraculously delivered. God snatched him as a stick out of the burning fire!

Abram thrown into fire to be killed - after converting his father Terah. Terah would not make any more idols.

---

[1] Many believe that Nimrod was also named 'Marduk,' whom scholars identify as the god of the Babylonian religions. His wife was Semiramis. They bore a child that is identified by some as the Egyptian *Osiris* and the Hindu *Vishnu*. See *The Two Babylons* by Alexander Hislop.

[2] Chaldea in Hebrew means 'demonic.'

CHAPTER FOURTEEN

ABRAM *& seers.*
saw many visitations

*"This is the account of
Terah . . . father of Abram"*

God spoke to Abram when was almost fifty years old. He was told to leave his country, his people, his father's household and go to the land God would reveal to him (Acts 7:1-3). Instead, we see Abram, his father, and his father's entire household going with him to a place called Haran. While in Haran, Terah died. Only after Terah died, did Abram leave and complete the journey.

Abram was slow to fully obey the word of the Lord. He compromised. He took all his clan with him to Haran. Abram didn't get very far . . . Haran was only a three days' journey from Ur. He stopped short of where he was called to go and he disobeyed by taking his support system with him. By failing to leave ALL behind, Abram ended up in Haran ('parched' or 'a dry place').

The name Terah means 'lagging behind' or 'delay.' There was a delay in God's plan for Abram because he took his father with him. This "delay" ended up being twenty-five years!

How often we lag behind in reaching the place of promise by taking with us what we should have left behind! The ties of human nature hindered the full response of Abram's heart. Terah is a picture of our old self (the old man) that must die before we can enter into our inheritance. Compromises will lead to delays in the unfolding of God's destiny for us!

Lot was to be left behind. Because he accompanied Abram, many sorrows in their relationship would later come. Abram set out for the land of his inheritance but settled far short of where God wanted to bring him. Eventually, Abram is forced to leave all his family, including Lot, and fulfill the plan of God.

"This is the account of Terah." It has been the purpose of the author of Genesis to bring us to this point. Everything up to now has been introductory in nature, incredibly informative and amazingly accurate, but only anticipating what is about to come. The SPIRITUAL SEED is placed in the heart of Abram. Chosen by the God of heaven, the story line now takes us into God's ultimate purposes.

If only we understood that we are called with a heavenly calling to an inheritance beyond description! This would keep us from finding satisfaction in having a "name" here on earth. How could we love the things of the world when we have been given *every spiritual bless-ing in heavenly places in Christ Jesus?* We must not delay or compromise in reaching the place God has destined for us.

It took DEATH to break the tie for Abram—it will take DEATH of self to break our tie to this life. The Cross of Christ is the place of separation FROM the world and TO the purposes of God. The same Cross that connects us to God separates us from the world (Gal. 6:14). Our "Terah" must die to move us forward into destiny.

In the New Testament, this failure of Abram is graciously overlooked. *"By faith Abraham, when called to go to a place he would later receive as his inheritance, obeyed and went, even though he did not know where he was going"* (Heb. 11:8). Grace had blotted out his sin.

Abraham's life is a story of *seven separations* he had to make. Each new separation brought new revelation. Each new revelation led to greater worship. Abraham would make a separation—then the Lord would speak to him—which prompted him to make an altar of worship. Here are the seven separations of Abraham's life. Each of them was a test of his faith. Each represents a parallel test for us in our own journey:

1. He had to leave his **COUNTRY** (Gen. 12:1). All that was familiar and comfortable had to be forsaken. The land governed by moon-worship (powers of darkness) must be abandoned. We must also leave the traditions that say, "You can go so far but no further."

2. He had to leave his father's **HOUSEHOLD** (Gen. 12:1). This deals with the closest ties of our heart. This represents both our natural and spiritual kindred. Sincere (but mistaken) family members will urge you not to leave and stay with them. Many within the church will refuse to let you go into the place of YOUR inheritance, seeking to keep you in their system.

3. Abram left **EGYPT** (Gen. 13:1). Egypt was only a stopping place, not his destination. Egypt is a type of the world-system full of the lusts of the flesh, the lusts of the eyes, and the pride of life. It is a place of bondage to man-pleasing and seeking prominence over others. To refuse to leave Egypt is to continue in bondage and servitude.

4. Abram eventually left **LOT** (Gen. 13:11). Lot was not a man of the Spirit, but of the flesh. He lived only from a carnal and worldly viewpoint. We must leave others behind to move forward into the call of God for our life. They are along for the ride but despise the responsibilities. They must be left behind. Family must be loved less than Christ (Luke 14:26).

5. Abram left his **DESIRE TO GET WEALTH** (Gen. 14:21-24). Great privilege and anointing will provide opportunity to get wealth, but all must be forsaken. God will provide unlimited provision upon those who seek first the kingdom of God. The man of faith must not be bought.

6. Abraham had to separate himself from **ISHMAEL** (Gen. 21:9-14). Ishmael was the product of the flesh, not the child of promise. Every manufactured attempt to bring forth the promise of God must be abandoned. Ishmael was Abraham's good idea, but not God's promise.

7. Abraham gave up his **ISAAC** (Gen. 22:1-14). This was his ultimate test of friendship with God. He had to give up even the promise God had fulfilled. God demands what he loved. This is worship in its purest sense.

This is only the beginning of the story of

The SPIRITUAL SEED

And the destiny God has for His people!

To Be Continued...

ABOUT THE AUTHOR

Dr. Brian Simmons has been in active ministry for thirty years. He and his wife, Candice, have served as tribal missionaries planting churches among the Kuna Indians, overseeing translation and consultant work. While in the jungle, they were visited by the Holy Spirit in a revival that brought many native people to salvation in Jesus Christ. This revival introduced the Simmons to the prophetic power of the end-time purposes of God. Brian has authored a number of books that focus on the purposes of God for this generation. They are convinced that God's Spirit will be poured out in revival power upon the nations of the earth, including the United States and New England, before the return of our Lord Jesus.

The passion of their ministry has been to equip this generation to become radical lovers of Jesus Christ. Their joy is mentoring young people, helping many find their place of ministry in the Body of Christ. Stairway Ministries has been established for that purpose. Brian is also the Senior Pastor of Gateway Christian Fellowship in West Haven, Connecticut where they make their home. They are blessed with three children and four grandchildren.

Other books by Dr. Brian Simmons:

GENESIS: *The Spiritual Seed & the Ways of God*
PRAYER PARTNERS WITH JESUS: *Secrets of Intercession*
SONG OF SONGS: *The Journey of the Bride*
DAVIDIC WORSHIP: *David, His Tabernacle & His Psalms*
ISAIAH: *The Prophet of Zion*

Author Contact Information

For more information on Stairway Ministries and a complete listing of their teaching materials, contact:

Stairway Ministries

P.O. Box 26512

West Haven, CT 06516

203-934-0880

Web Address: www.StairwayMinistries.org

Email: stairwayministry@hotmail.com